FORGIVING YOUR FATHER

21 Day Journal To Mend Hearts And Find Your Inner Peace On The Path To Reconciliation

Blending Our Love, Maryland

Copyright © 2023 by Tuniscia Okeke

Cover Design:

Published 2023

Library of Congress Cataloging-in-Publication Data

ISBN: 978-1-962748-24-7 (Print)

ISBN: 978-1-962748-25-4 (eBook)

Printed in the United States of America

FORGIVING YOUR FATHER

21 Day Journal To Mend Hearts And Find Your Inner Peace On The Path To Reconciliation

TUNISCIA OKEKE

BLENDING OUR LOVE, INC.

DEDICATION

I forgive you.

Table of Contents

Paying It Forward

I'm sharing this message as the author of this 21-day journal on forgiveness, not just with words on these pages but with a story that has shaped my life's purpose. As I embark on this journey with you, I want to share the deeply personal and transformative experiences that led me to write, edit, and self-publish 35 books on forgiveness in less than a year.

My forgiveness journey began when I was 24, a pivotal age when life often feels like an open book, brimming with hope and dreams. Then, my mother called me on a seemingly ordinary Monday morning, and with those words, she unraveled the narrative of my life. She revealed that the man I had believed to be my father for all those years was, in fact, not my biological father.

The weight of that revelation was crushing. It was as if the ground beneath me had shifted, leaving me unsteady and disoriented. But what shook me to my core was not the revelation itself but the sudden rupture of trust in my mother—the person I had always looked up to as a paragon of love, trustworthiness, and honesty.

In the wake of this revelation, I spiraled into a deep pit of resentment, anger, and pain. I grappled with a profound sense of betrayal and felt adrift in a sea of unanswered questions. It was a turbulent period in my life, and for 17 long years, I carried the heavy burden of unforgiveness.

Then, something remarkable happened that would alter the course of my life forever. I noticed a pattern in my relationship with my children. They treated me with a lack of respect and love, leaving me bewildered and hurt. In desperation, I turned to prayer one day, seeking answers from a higher source.

God's voice whispered into my heart in that sacred space of prayer and introspection, revealing a profound truth: "I taught them how to love me by the way I loved my mother."

Those words struck me like lightning, piercing through the fog of my confusion. It was an awakening—a profound realization that, in my quest for revenge against my mother, I had unwittingly passed on the energy of resentment to my children. I had normalized my hurtful behaviors as the way we should treat our mothers.

On my 40th birthday, I consciously confronted my soul's deepest and darkest corners. I embarked on a journey of healing, self-forgiveness, and forgiveness of my mother. My primary motivation was to restore my relationship with my children and teach them how to pass on healing, love, and forgiveness to their children.

That six-year odyssey of healing was transformative beyond measure. It led me to write 35 journals, each addressing a facet of forgiveness and healing I encountered on my journey. These journals became my way of reaching out to others grappling with their forgiveness journeys.

Today, I extend a heartfelt invitation to you to embark on this 21-day journey with me. Just as my healing journey began with a single journal, this journal can be your compass for forgiveness, healing, and growth.

I send you loving energy as you navigate through the complexities of your forgiveness journey, and I hope these pages serve as a guiding light toward wholeness and inner peace.

With love and compassion,

Tuniscia O

FOREWORD

Dear Dynamic Reader,

I am grateful for allowing me to join your journey through this journal, "Forgiving Your Father." It takes immense courage to embark on such a deeply personal exploration, and I commend you for taking this significant step towards healing and growth.

The relationship we share with our fathers can be complex, layered with emotions, memories, and experiences that have shaped us in profound ways. It's a relationship that can influence our self-esteem, our ability to trust, and our capacity to love and forgive.

As the author of this journal, I want you to know that I stand beside you, not as an expert with all the answers, but as a fellow traveler on this path of forgiveness and healing. I have my own experiences and struggles, and I understand the challenges that can arise when we confront the wounds of the past.

This journal allows you to reflect, release, and reclaim your power. It's not about pushing you to forgive quickly or forget the pain but rather about providing the tools, insights, and support you need to navigate this journey at your own pace.

As you open these pages daily, remember you are not alone. Your feelings, whether anger, sadness, confusion, or hope, are valid. This journal is a safe haven for all those emotions, where you can explore them without judgment.

Through these 21 days, we will delve into the layers of forgiveness. We will explore the complexities of your relationship with your father and guide you toward a place of healing. But always remember, you control this process and can choose what feels suitable for you.

I encourage you to be gentle with yourself and to celebrate your progress, no matter how small it may seem. Each step you take towards forgiveness is a victory, and each moment of self-compassion is a triumph.

Thank you for entrusting me with this part of your journey. Together, we will navigate the path of forgiveness, and I believe that, in the end, you will emerge confident, more resilient, and with a heart full of healing and love.

With warmth and support,

Tuniscia O

Healing the Heart

Introduction

I n the labyrinth of life, we often find ourselves entangled in the threads of our past—past experiences, relationships, and memories that shape the tapestry of our existence. Among these threads, our relationship with our father is one of the most intricate and profound. This relationship has the power to weave threads of love, support, and understanding, but it can also thread in challenges, pain, and unresolved emotions.

A Journey of Forgiveness, Healing, and Growth explores the profound process of forgiving our fathers, releasing resentment and blame, and taking accountability for our lives. In these pages, we will delve into the depths of the human heart, navigating through the complexities of emotions that arise from father-child relationships. We will embark on a journey of self-discovery, acceptance, and transformation, understanding that healing begins when we release the grip of the past and embrace the power of forgiveness.

The story of forgiveness is an ancient one, etched into the histories of cultures and societies across the globe. It is a narrative that transcends time and resonates with the universal longing for liberation from the chains of bitterness and pain. Within these pages, we will uncover the profound truth that forgiveness isn't condoning hurtful actions but a radical act of self-love and empowerment. It is an opportunity to break free from resentment and blame and reclaim our power to shape our lives.

Threads Of Our Past

These threads are not just memories but the emotions, beliefs, and experiences that have influenced our relationships, particularly our connections with our fathers. By embarking on a journey to understand these threads, we embark on a path of profound self-discovery.

Some threads may be woven with love and warmth, creating strong bonds of trust and affection with our fathers. Others may be laced with pain, misunderstanding, or abandonment, causing us to question our self-worth and leaving wounds that require healing.

Acknowledging these threads is an act of courage and self-compassion. It's an invitation to look deep within ourselves and confront the raw emotions that may have long remained hidden. Through this process, we gain insight into why we feel the way we do and why we react to certain situations as we do.

As we trace these threads, we untangle the knots of resentment, blame, or hurt that may have entwined our hearts. We start to see that our fathers, like all individuals, are complex beings with flaws and struggles.

Ultimately, understanding the threads of our past is the first step toward forgiveness and healing. It allows us to separate the person from the actions, empathize with their journey, and control our emotional well-being.

In this exploration, we empower ourselves to rewrite the narrative to choose how we want to engage with our fathers in the present and the future. It's a transformative journey of self-discovery, forgiveness, and growth, and it begins with unraveling the threads of our past.

The journey towards healing and growth begins with understanding the threads that have woven our past. We will explore the various experiences, memories, and emotions that have shaped our perceptions of our fathers. By acknowledging these threads, we lay the foundation for unraveling our relationships' complexities and uncovering our resentments' origins.

The Power of Forgiveness

Forgiveness is a profound and multifaceted concept that holds the power to reshape our lives in remarkable ways. At its core, forgiveness is an act of courage and self-liberation, not a sign of weakness. The journey transcends hurt and resentment, leading us toward healing and growth.

Forgiving doesn't mean we condone the actions that hurt or forget the pain inflicted upon us. It's about reclaiming our own power and emotional well-being. When we forgive, we release the heavy burden of anger, resentment, and bitterness that weigh us down. We acknowledge that holding onto these negative emotions only continues to hurt us.

The transformational power of forgiveness lies in its ability to free us from the chains of the past. It allows us to break the cycle of pain and suffering, paving the way for inner peace and emotional freedom. By forgiving, we take control of our narrative, no longer allowing the actions of others to define us.

Furthermore, forgiveness can mend broken relationships and build bridges between individuals. It fosters understanding and empathy, opening the door to reconciliation and rebuilding trust. It can also profoundly impact our physical and mental health, reducing stress and promoting overall well-being.

In essence, forgiveness is a gift we give ourselves. It's a journey of self-discovery, compassion, and empowerment. By embracing the power of forgiveness, we heal our wounds and create a brighter and more harmonious future for ourselves and those around us.

Dive into the concept of forgiveness, examining its multifaceted nature. Find the strength to forgive because forgiveness is not a sign of weakness but a profound act of courage and self-liberation. Explore the transformational power of forgiveness and how it can reshape our emotional landscape.

The Art of Letting Go

It's the process of consciously and willingly releasing resentment and blame, recognizing that holding onto these negative emotions perpetuates our suffering.

When we carry the weight of past grievances, we inadvertently tie ourselves to the pain of the past. It's like dragging a heavy anchor through life's waters, hindering our progress and preventing us from fully embracing the present. Letting go is about setting down that anchor and allowing ourselves to float freely.

Mindfulness plays a pivotal role in this process. Mindfulness practices teach us to observe our thoughts and emotions without judgment. This allows us to detach from the grip of our past hurts and create space for healing and growth. We become aware of the stories we've woven around our pain and can begin to unravel them.

Letting go doesn't mean we forget or condone the actions that hurt us. It means we choose not to be defined by them any longer. It's a courageous act of reclaiming our power and steering our emotional ship.

In the art of letting go, we discover liberation and inner peace. We allow forgiveness to flourish, paving the way for a brighter, more joyful future. It's a beautiful and empowering journey that leads us toward healing and growth, one step at a time.

Releasing resentment and blame is an essential step on the path to forgiveness. The art of letting go and growing to understand that holding onto negative emotions only perpetuates our suffering. Through mindfulness practices, we will learn to detach from our past grievances and create space for healing and growth.

Taking Charge of Our Lives

It begins by redirecting our focus from blame, which keeps us anchored in the past, to accountability, propelling us toward a brighter future.

In the journey of accountability, we acknowledge that we cannot change the past or the actions of others. However, we can change our response and our outlook. We recognize that our reactions, choices, and decisions are our own, and they shape our path ahead. This awareness is liberating because it reminds us that we have the power to shape our destiny.

We become the authors of our stories by taking responsibility for our lives. We no longer allow external circumstances or past events to define us. Instead, we seize the reins and steer our lives in our desired direction.

Accountability doesn't mean denying the impact of external factors or past experiences; it means choosing how we respond to them. It's a declaration of self-empowerment and resilience. It's about learning from our mistakes, overcoming challenges, and celebrating our successes.

As we embrace accountability, we discover a sense of purpose and agency. We become architects of our future, shaping a life that aligns with our values and aspirations. It's a journey of self-discovery and personal growth, inviting us to step confidently into the life we want to create.

Accountability is a cornerstone of personal growth. Let's shift our focus from blame to accountability, acknowledging that while we cannot change the past, we can shape our future. We reclaim the power to define our narrative and shape our destiny by taking responsibility for our lives.

Embracing Self-Compassion

In forgiving our fathers, we must remember that we are not perfect, and neither are they. Self-compassion invites us to acknowledge our humanity, complete with flaws and imperfections. It reminds us that it's okay to make mistakes, to feel hurt, and to struggle with forgiveness.

By nurturing self-compassion, we create a nurturing environment for healing. We recognize that healing is not a linear path but a journey filled with ups and downs. When we treat ourselves compassionately, we offer solace to the wounded parts of our hearts.

Self-compassion practices, such as mindfulness and self-kindness, become tools for emotional well-being. These practices help us navigate the emotions that arise during the forgiveness process and provide us with a safe space to process our feelings.

Furthermore, self-compassion fosters resilience. It strengthens us to keep moving forward, even when forgiveness seems daunting. It reminds us that we are worthy of love and healing and encourages us to be patient and gentle with ourselves.

In essence, embracing self-compassion is a profound act of self-love. It supports our journey toward forgiveness and enriches our well-being, allowing us to navigate life's challenges with extraordinary grace and resilience.

Forgiving our fathers involves forgiving ourselves as well. Get curious about the importance of self-compassion, learning to treat ourselves with the same kindness and understanding we extend to others. Through self-compassion practices, we will nurture our emotional well-being and create a nurturing environment for healing.

The Path To Healing

Mindfulness is a powerful companion on this path. It invites us to be fully present in each moment, to observe our thoughts and emotions without judgment. Mindfulness teaches us to be kind to ourselves, fostering self-compassion and self-awareness.

Therapy is a crucial guide on our healing journey. It offers a safe and supportive space to explore our experiences, uncover deep-seated wounds, and develop tools for healing and growth. It's an opportunity to get vulnerable and share our stories with a trusted guide.

Creative expression becomes a form of catharsis. Through art, writing, or other creative outlets, we give voice to our innermost feelings and experiences. This act of creation becomes a bridge to understanding and self-discovery.

As we tread this path to healing, we take practical steps to mend our wounded hearts and find a sense of wholeness. We learn to set boundaries, practice self-care, and cultivate resilience. It's a journey filled with challenges and triumphs, but with each step, we move closer to a place of emotional well-being and inner peace.

Ultimately, the path to healing is a beautiful odyssey of self-discovery and self-love. It's an invitation to embrace our authenticity, nurture our wounds, and emerge stronger, wiser, and more whole.

Healing is a holistic journey encompassing the mind, body, and spirit. Enjoy the journey as you delve into various healing modalities—mindfulness, therapy, creative expression, and more—that can guide us toward emotional liberation. Get vulnerable as you take practical steps to mend our wounded hearts and find a sense of wholeness.

Reclaiming Our Power

Through forgiveness, we rewrite our narratives. We move from victimhood to empowerment, recognizing that we can shape our destinies. It's about taking the reins of our lives, no longer allowing the actions of others or past events to define us.

Healing becomes our anchor on this journey. It's a process of mending our wounded hearts, nurturing our emotional well-being, and finding a sense of wholeness. Healing allows us to shed the heavy baggage of resentment and pain, making room for growth and positivity.

In moments of empowerment and transformation, we realize our past does not bind us. We are not limited by the wounds we've carried. Instead, we rise above them, more resilient and confident than before.

Reclaiming our power means embracing self-compassion, setting healthy boundaries, and making choices that align with our values and aspirations. It's a journey of inner strength and a deep sense of self-worth.

Ultimately, reclaiming our power creates a future filled with positivity, growth, and self-empowerment. It's a journey that showcases the remarkable capacity of the human spirit to heal, forgive, and rise above adversity.

We will encounter moments of empowerment and transformation as we progress. Rewrite and reclaim your power through forgiveness and healing, showcasing that you can rise above your past and create a future filled with positivity and growth.

Unveiling

As we move forward, we witness the unraveling of old, limiting patterns that no longer serve us. These patterns may have kept us tethered to resentment and blame. Letting go of them is an act of liberation, a release from the chains that bound us to the past.

In their place, a new tapestry is woven with healing, growth, and forgiveness threads. This tapestry reflects our inner transformation, a testament to our commitment to self-discovery and self-compassion.

We honor the human spirit's resilience in this unveiling process. It recognizes our ability to endure, learn, and grow from adversity. It's proof that we can forge a new path, not defined by the wounds of the past, but by our intentions and choices in the present.

The new tapestry is a testament to our capacity to heal and forgive others and ourselves. It's a work of art representing our journey toward wholeness and emotional well-being. As we stand in awe of this evolving masterpiece, we embrace the power of transformation and the beauty of the human spirit's enduring strength.

As you navigate forward, celebrate the unraveling of old patterns, the release of resentment and blame, and the emergence of a new tapestry of healing, growth, and forgiveness. Honor the resilience of the human spirit and the capacity to forge a new path, not defined by the past but by your intentions and choices.

Nurturing Healing from Childhood Wounds

In the quiet corners of our hearts lie the remnants of childhood wounds—impressions left by experiences, relationships, and memories. These wounds, often carried into adulthood, can cast a shadow over our well-being and influence our perceptions of ourselves and the world around us. For those whose relationships with their fathers were marked by pain, neglect, or abandonment, the journey of healing these wounds can be profound and transformative.

These lingering wounds can shadow our well-being, affecting how we perceive ourselves and the world. In cases where our relationships with our fathers were marred by pain, neglect, or abandonment, the healing journey takes on a profound and transformative dimension.

Mindful journaling and self-reflection are potent tools in this process. They provide a safe and sacred space to explore the depths of our emotions, confront the scars of the past, and understand how these wounds have influenced our present lives.

Through mindful journaling, we can begin to untangle the intricate threads of our experiences, shedding light on the roots of our pain. Self-reflection allows us to observe our thoughts and emotions with kindness, fostering self-compassion and self-awareness.

As we navigate this healing journey, we honor the resilience of the human spirit. It's an exploration of our capacity to heal and transform, a testament to our ability to release the grip of the past and embrace a future filled with healing, growth, and inner peace.

The Power of Mindful Journaling

Journaling is a gentle yet profound practice that invites us to reflect with intention and compassion. It is a sacred space where we can release our thoughts, emotions, and memories onto paper, allowing them to unfold without judgment. Through mindful journaling, we create a safe container to explore our feelings, memories, and wounds with kindness and understanding.

Begin by finding a quiet space where you can sit comfortably. Take a few deep breaths, allowing yourself to arrive fully in the present moment. As you open your journal, set an intention to approach this practice with a heart full of self-love and curiosity. Let go of expectations and permit yourself to explore your emotions without criticism.

This practice is an invitation to engage in self-reflection with intention and compassion. It encourages us to enter into a partnership with our minds and listen to our hearts' whispers without judgment. Mindful journaling is a practice of presence, allowing us to fully inhabit the here and now as we pour our thoughts onto paper.

In the quiet solitude of a chosen space, we embark on this journey of self-exploration. We begin by centering ourselves, grounding in the present moment through deep breaths and conscious awareness. As we open our journal, we approach this process with self-love and curiosity, free from rigid expectations or criticism.

Through mindful journaling, we foster self-compassion. We become our confidants, offering solace and understanding to the wounded parts of ourselves. We create a bridge between our conscious and unconscious minds, unraveling the mysteries of our emotions and beliefs.

Ultimately, the power of mindful journaling lies in its capacity to illuminate our inner world and facilitate personal growth. It is a practice that supports our emotional well-being, encourages self-awareness, and empowers us to navigate life's challenges with resilience and grace.

Navigating The Landscape
Of Childhood Wounds

Navigating the landscape of childhood wounds is a courageous step toward healing. In this sacred space of reflection and self-discovery, we embark on a journey into the depths of our past, where memories of our father reside.

As we put pen to paper, we create a bridge to our childhood, recalling both the cherished moments and the challenges. It's an opportunity to revisit the chapters of our lives, to remember the laughter, lessons, love, and moments of pain or neglect.

Crucially, this process is not about assigning blame but about healing. It's a gentle exploration of the feelings that arise—anger, sadness, longing, or perhaps even glimpses of joy. In this judgment-free zone, we can express ourselves authentically, releasing our lingering emotions.

By confronting these memories and emotions, we begin to untangle the threads of our past, unraveling the patterns that may have influenced our relationships and beliefs. It's a transformative journey that empowers us to release the grip of childhood wounds and embrace the freedom of forgiveness and self-compassion.

In this healing space, we honor our resilience and capacity for growth. We reclaim our power to shape our narratives and find solace in the understanding that our past need not define our future. As we navigate the landscape of childhood wounds, we pave the way for a brighter, more emotionally liberated tomorrow.

Reflect on the memories and emotions linked to your father from childhood. Allow yourself to recall both positive and challenging experiences. As you write, remember that this is a healing space, not blame. Gently explore the feelings that arise—anger, sadness, longing, or perhaps even glimpses of joy. Your journal is a judgment-free zone, allowing you to express yourself authentically.

Releasing the Blame

Forgiving one's father can be a profound and often challenging journey, especially when there is a history of pain and disappointment. "Releasing the blame" is an essential step on this path to healing and reconciliation.

Blame, like heavy chains, can tether us to our past, preventing us from moving forward in our lives and relationships. When forgiving your father, it's crucial to recognize that releasing blame isn't about condoning any wrongdoings but about freeing yourself from the burden of resentment and anger.

To release the blame, begin by acknowledging your feelings and allowing yourself to express them in a healthy way, whether through journaling, therapy, or conversations with a trusted friend. It's essential to validate your emotions and honor your pain.

Next, try to understand your father's perspective and the circumstances that may have influenced his actions. This doesn't excuse any hurtful behavior but can offer insight into the complexity of human experiences.

Practice self-compassion by recognizing that forgiveness is a gift you give to yourself. As you release blame, you create space for healing, personal growth, and the potential for a more peaceful relationship with your father. Remember that forgiveness is a process, and it may take time, but it is a powerful step toward liberation and emotional well-being.

Confronting Memories

Confronting the memories of the past when considering forgiveness for your father is a complex and deeply emotional journey. It's a process that requires you to navigate through both the struggles and the cherished moments that have shaped your relationship.

The memories of pain and disappointment may weigh heavily on your heart, making it difficult to move on. It's natural to feel hurt, angry, and even betrayed by a father figure who may not have lived up to your expectations or who may have caused you emotional wounds. These emotions can create a barrier to forgiveness.

However, it's equally important to remember the moments of joy, love, and connection you shared with your father. Reflecting on the good times can help you see the full spectrum of your relationship and acknowledge that it wasn't entirely defined by pain.

Moving on from the past is challenging because it means letting go of the familiar, even if it's painful. It's a process of finding a new perspective, one that doesn't deny the difficulties but also recognizes the potential for growth and healing. It's about freeing yourself from the grip of past hurts while honoring the lessons and experiences that have made you who you are today.

Confronting these memories, both the struggles and the good times is an essential step in the journey toward forgiveness and healing. It allows you to make peace with your past and open the door to a more peaceful and liberated future.

Nurturing A Sanctuary For Emotional Healing

Creating a healthy emotional healing space is like tending to the garden of your heart, where the seeds of forgiveness and understanding can flourish. It's a deliberate act of self-care that not only impacts how you relate to your father but ripples into every corner of your life and relationships, especially with the men who have played pivotal roles.

Your relationship with your father, whether strained or supportive, has left imprints on how you perceive and interact with men in general. If there have been wounds or misunderstandings, it can shape a lens of caution, mistrust, or fear. Alternatively, if your father has been a source of love and guidance, it can set a positive standard for the men you welcome into your life.

Creating a nurturing emotional space means acknowledging the impact of these experiences and allowing yourself to heal from any unresolved issues. It involves self-reflection, self-compassion, and seeking support when needed. As you cultivate this inner sanctuary, you're better equipped to navigate relationships with men in a healthier, more balanced way.

The healing process opens the door to clearer communication, empathy, and the ability to set healthy boundaries in all your relationships. It allows you to relate to men from a place of strength and self-assuredness, rather than being burdened by the weight of past emotional baggage. Ultimately, nurturing this space for emotional healing enhances your capacity for love, understanding, and meaningful connections in all aspects of your life.

Story Time

Once upon a time, in a quaint little town, a man named Daniel lived. Daniel had carried a heavy burden throughout his life – the weight of unresolved anger and resentment towards his father. For years, the pain of his past had cast a dark shadow over his present, affecting his relationships, self-esteem, and overall happiness.

One sunny morning, as Daniel sipped his tea and gazed out at the world outside his window, he felt a deep longing for something different. He yearned for peace and understanding, not just in his relationship with his father but within himself as well. Then, he decided to embark on a journey of self-reflection.

The journey began with Daniel acknowledging the pain he had carried for so long. He allowed himself to feel the anger and hurt that had festered within him. Instead of pushing these emotions away, he welcomed them as part of his experience. He realized that he was taking the first step toward healing by acknowledging his pain.

As Daniel delved deeper into his self-reflection, he started to understand the incredible resilience that had been his guiding light. He recognized the moments of strength and wisdom he had gained through the challenges he faced growing up. He saw that his father, flawed as he was, had also played a role in shaping the person he had become.

With newfound clarity, Daniel decided to reach out to his father. He penned a heartfelt letter, not as an accusation but as an expression of his desire for understanding and healing. He acknowledged that he and his father had made mistakes in the past, and he was ready to move forward with an open heart.

To his surprise, his father responded with a letter of his own. In it, he expressed his regret for the pain he had caused and shared his struggles and regrets. Their exchange of letters became a bridge to reconciliation, a pathway to forgiveness.

Daniel and his father decided to meet in person, and when they did, tears flowed freely, but this time, they were tears of release and relief. They embraced one another, not just as father and son, but as two flawed individuals who had found forgiveness and understanding.

As time passed, Daniel's relationship with his father deepened. They began to build new memories, free from the burdens of the past. But perhaps even more importantly, Daniel's relationship with himself transformed. He had learned that "Embracing Compassionate Self-Reflection" was a profound act of self-healing and self-discovery.

Daniel had unlocked a treasure within himself – the ability to forgive, not just his father, but himself as well. He had found that in forgiving others, we often find the greatest gift of all: the freedom to live in the present, unburdened by the pain of the past.

Cultivating Release
Through Journaling

R elease is a profound journey of inner transformation, and mindful journaling serves as a powerful tool to navigate this path. This intentional practice provides us with a safe and sacred space for self-reflection, allowing us to confront the resentment and blame that may have entwined our hearts with the past.

In the pages of our journal, we embark on a voyage of self-discovery and healing. Here, forgiveness is not about excusing hurtful actions or betrayals; instead, it's a liberation of our own souls from the weight of anger and bitterness. Through mindful journaling, we examine our wounds, acknowledging the pain and suffering they have caused us.

As we put pen to paper, we confront our emotions head-on, giving them the attention and validation they deserve. We ask ourselves tough questions, such as why we're holding onto these grudges and what they are costing us in terms of inner peace and growth. This self-inquiry unveils insights and perspectives we might not have otherwise discovered.

By journaling with mindfulness and intention, we gradually unravel the knots of resentment and blame, making space for forgiveness to bloom. We realize that forgiving is an act of self-compassion, allowing us to heal and move forward unburdened by the past. Through this transformative process, we not only release others from our grip but, most importantly, ourselves, setting our spirits free to embrace a brighter, more peaceful future.

Inviting Healing and Transformation

As you journal, notice shifts in your perspective and emotions. Allow yourself to witness your growth and transformation. Celebrate moments of self-compassion, forgiveness, and release. Your journal becomes a living testimony of your healing journey—one that serves as a reminder of your resilience and capacity to heal.

Through mindful journaling, you become the witness to your growth and transformation. It's like tracing the delicate tendrils of a vine as they slowly reach for the light. Each entry in your journal represents a step forward, a moment of self-awareness, or an act of self-compassion.

Celebrate these moments of self-compassion, forgiveness, and release you encounter on your journey. They are like small, radiant stars in the night sky, guiding you towards emotional liberation and inner peace. They remind you of the resilience and healing capacity that reside within you.

Your journal becomes a living testimony of your healing journey—a chronicle of your triumphs, no matter how small they seem. It serves as a reminder that healing is not a linear path but a profound transformation that takes time and patience. It shows your courage, vulnerability, and commitment to self-discovery and growth.

In essence, inviting healing and transformation through journaling is an act of self-love and empowerment. It's an affirmation of your worthiness of healing, and it empowers you to navigate life's challenges with grace and resilience. Your journal is a cherished companion on this journey, helping you write your story of healing, growth, and renewal.

Creating A Ritual of Mindful Journaling

Set aside daily or weekly to make mindful journaling a regular practice. Create a ritual that honors this space of reflection—a cozy corner, a soothing cup of tea, or calming music. Approach your journal with an open heart, ready to embrace whatever emerges.

Remember, healing from childhood wounds takes time and patience. Be gentle with yourself as you navigate the layers of your emotions and memories. Journaling becomes a cherished companion on this journey, offering solace, insight, and transformation. Through this practice, you can reclaim your narrative, release the grip of the past, and nurture a sense of wholeness that allows you to enter the present with a healing and thriving heart.

Journaling your meditative thoughts is a powerful practice that bridges the gap between your inner reflections and tangible expressions on paper. It's a way to capture the essence of your mindfulness journey, cultivating self-awareness, healing, and personal growth. Here are some best practices to enhance your experience of journaling meditative thoughts:

Create a Sacred Space

Find a quiet, comfortable space where you won't be disturbed. This environment helps you disconnect from distractions and immerse yourself fully in journaling.

Creating a sacred space for your journaling practice is a beautiful act of self-care and self-nurturing. It's an invitation to honor your thoughts and emotions, to give them the attention they deserve. In this serene environment, you can disconnect from the outside world and immerse yourself fully in self-reflection and healing. It's your sanctuary, where your words flow freely, your emotions find expression, and your healing journey unfolds. So, find that quiet, comfortable space where you won't be disturbed, and let it become the canvas on which you paint the landscape of your inner world.

Set An Intention

Before you begin, set an intention for your journaling session. Decide on the purpose of your writing—whether it's to release negative emotions, gain insights, or seek clarity on a particular issue.

Setting an intention for your journaling session is like charting a course for your inner voyage. It provides focus and purpose to your writing, guiding your thoughts and emotions in a meaningful direction. Whether you seek to release, gain, or clarify, your intention becomes the compass that leads you toward self-discovery and healing. So, before you put pen to paper, take a moment to decide your purpose. Your intention is the map that will help you navigate the landscapes of your inner world with clarity and purpose.

Breathe and Ground Yourself

Take a few deep breaths to center yourself. Ground your awareness in the present moment by focusing on your breath or the sensations in your body.

Breathe, dear friend. Inhale the serenity of the present moment and exhale any tension or worries. Ground yourself in the now, feeling the gentle rhythm of your breath. This simple mindfulness connects you to the calm within, providing a steady foundation for your journaling journey.

Start With A Meditative Practice

Engage in a brief meditative practice to settle your mind. This could involve mindfulness breathing, body scan, or simply observing your thoughts without attachment.

Begin your journaling journey with a meditative practice. Inhale serenity, exhale distractions. As you settle your mind, you create a tranquil canvas for your thoughts and emotions. Whether breathing mindfulness or observing thoughts without attachment, this practice nurtures the stillness within, guiding your journaling with clarity and presence.

Let the Words Flow

Open your journal and let your thoughts flow onto the pages. Write freely without concern for grammar, spelling, or structure. Let your thoughts spill onto the paper as they arise.

Let the words flow like a river, unrestrained and unfiltered. This is your sacred space, a canvas for your thoughts and emotions to dance freely. Don't worry about perfection; just let them spill onto the paper, forming the mosaic of your inner world. In this flow, you'll discover insights and healing.

Be Honest and Authentic

Your journal is a private space to express your innermost thoughts without judgment. Be honest and authentic in your writing, allowing yourself to confront difficult emotions and celebrate positive insights.

In the pages of your journal, authenticity is your guiding light. Embrace honesty as your ally, a trusted confidant. It's a sanctuary where you can confront your deepest emotions without fear or judgment. Celebrate your authenticity as you unveil the layers of your inner world, and in this honesty, find the path to healing and self-discovery.

Explore Your Emotions

Acknowledge and explore the emotions that arise during your meditation. Describe the feelings you experienced, whether they were calming, challenging, or transformative.

In the gentle embrace of meditation, explore the intricate landscape of your emotions. Acknowledge each feeling, whether calm or challenging, as a part of your unique journey. Describe them honestly and without reservation. Through this exploration, you illuminate the path to self-understanding, growth, and transformation.

Reflect on Insights

If any insights or realizations emerged during meditation, elaborate on them in your journal. Reflect on how they relate to your life and how they can guide your actions.

As you journal, honor the insights that have graced your meditation. Dive into their depths and explore their significance in the context of your life. Reflect on how these revelations can illuminate your path, guiding your actions with newfound wisdom and clarity. Embrace the gift of self-discovery.

Gratitude and Self-Compassion

Incorporate gratitude and self-compassion into your journaling practice—express appreciation for the opportunity to meditate and be present with your thoughts. Extend kindness and understanding to yourself, especially if challenging emotions surface.

Embrace gratitude and self-compassion as your loyal companions on this journey. Express thankfulness for the gift of meditation, for the chance to be present with your thoughts. Shower yourself with kindness and understanding, especially when challenging emotions emerge. In these acts of grace, you nurture the soil for growth and healing.

Set Intentions for the Day

As you journal, set intentions for the rest of your day. Reflect on how your meditative insights influence your actions, decisions, and interactions.

As you bid farewell to your journaling session, set intentions like precious jewels for the day ahead. Contemplate how the insights from your meditation can shape your actions, decisions, and interactions. In these intentions, you infuse purpose and mindfulness into your day, sowing the seeds of a harmonious and fulfilling journey ahead.

Review and Reflect

Periodically review your journal entries to observe patterns, track your progress, and witness your growth over time. This reflection can offer valuable insights into your mindfulness journey.

In the tapestry of your journal entries lies a treasure trove of insights. Periodically, take time to review and reflect. Observe the patterns that emerge, track your progress, and witness the beautiful evolution of your mindfulness journey. In this reflection, you discover the threads of growth that weave through your life.

Be Consistent

Consistency in journaling meditative thoughts is like tending to the garden of your inner world. The steady watering nourishes the seeds of mindfulness, allowing them to grow into vibrant flowers of self-discovery and healing.

Make it a regular practice tailored to your unique needs and preferences. Whether daily, weekly or any frequency that feels right for you, the key is establishing a rhythm you can sustain. Consistency provides the structure that helps you stay committed to this nurturing act of self-care.

You'll witness the gradual transformation of your inner landscape through consistent journaling. It's a journey of self-awareness, where you'll uncover patterns, gain insights, and develop a deeper connection with yourself. Like a skilled navigator, your journal guides you through the currents of your thoughts and emotions, leading you toward the shores of inner peace.

Furthermore, consistency allows you to track your progress over time. It's a record of your personal growth, a testament to your resilience, and a source of inspiration when faced with challenges. It reminds you of the strength and wisdom you've cultivated on your mindfulness journey.

So, embrace consistency in your journaling practice as a gift to yourself. It's an investment in your well-being, a sanctuary for your thoughts, and a pathway to greater self-awareness. Through the steady commitment to this practice, you'll find that your journal becomes a trusted companion on your quest for inner peace and self-discovery.

Consistency is critical to reaping the full benefits of journaling meditative thoughts. Make it a regular practice, whether daily, weekly, or as often as feels right for you.

Journaling your meditative thoughts is an act of self-care and self-discovery. It's a space to explore your inner landscape, nurture mindfulness, and cultivate a deeper connection with yourself. By embracing these best practices, you'll find that your journal becomes a treasure trove of wisdom, insights, and a testament to your journey towards greater self-awareness and inner peace.

Journal Your Way Forward

With just 15 minutes a day, your journal becomes a catalyst for profound transformation. Each entry is a step closer to understanding, healing, and growth. Through daily journaling, you harness the power to create massive positive change in your life, unlocking your true potential and embracing a brighter future.

Here's a list of tips on how to successfully journal for 15 minutes per day:

Set a Consistent Time

Choose a specific time each day for your journaling practice, such as in the morning or before bedtime, to establish a routine.

Create a Comfortable Space

Find a quiet and comfortable place where you can focus without distractions.

Start With A Goal

Determine what you want to achieve through journaling. Are you seeking self-reflection, gratitude, or problem-solving? Having a purpose helps guide your entries.

Set A Timer

Allocate 15 minutes using a timer to keep yourself on track and prevent overthinking.

Write Freely

Don't worry about grammar or structure. Let your thoughts flow naturally, even if they seem disorganized at first.

Focus On Feelings

Journaling is a space to express your emotions honestly. Describe how you feel and why you feel that way.

Reflect On The Day

Summarize your day or highlight significant moments, whether positive or challenging.

Practice Gratitude

Dedicate a portion of your journaling time to list things you're grateful for. This can boost your mood and perspective.

Set Goals And Intentions

Use journaling to set daily goals or intentions, helping you stay focused and accountable.

Review And Revise

Periodically revisit your previous entries to track your progress, identify patterns, and gain insights.

Be Patient With Yourself

If you miss a day or don't have much to write about, don't be too hard on yourself. Journaling is a personal practice, and consistency over time is more important than perfection in each entry.

Remember, journaling is a flexible and personal practice, so adapt these tips to suit your preferences and needs. The key is to make it a regular habit that supports your well-being and self-discovery.

So, pick up your pen and let it dance across the pages. Let the ink weave a tapestry of healing and empowerment—an intimate conversation with yourself that leads to renewal. Embrace the transformative power of journaling and step into a future where you stand tall, unburdened by the weight of wounds, and radiate with the radiance of self-love and the beauty of your unique journey.

I Forgive You For Not Knowing How To Love Me

Forgiveness Inner Reflection of the Day

Facing the reality that my father didn't know how to love me in the way I desired has been a challenging yet liberating journey. I held onto expectations for so long and hoped his love would fill a void within me. But as I reflect deeply, I understand that he might not have known how to express love in the way I needed.

Acknowledging this truth is not about blaming him or seeking excuses. It's about recognizing the limitations he might have had due to his own experiences and upbringing. It's about understanding that his actions reflected not my worth but his struggles.

In this reflection, I find both sorrow and release. I allow myself to mourn the loss of the love I yearned for while embracing the opportunity to heal. I release the expectations that tied me to disappointment, resentment and hurt. By acknowledging his limitations, I free myself from the weight of unfulfilled desires.

I choose to nurture self-compassion and self-love. I acknowledge that my longing for love is valid and natural. Through forgiveness, I detach my self-worth from his actions, recognizing that I deserve love regardless of his ability.

As I face this reality, I find empowerment in my capacity to heal and grow. I can now focus on filling that void with self-love, nurturing relationships, and positive experiences. I am no longer held hostage by what was lacking; instead, I channel my energy towards building a foundation of love within myself.

This reflection allows me to reframe my narrative. It's not about blaming or victimizing but about understanding and releasing. I take control of my emotional well-being by accepting what was and embracing what can be. I cultivate forgiveness for my father and myself as I release the pain that no longer serves me. With this newfound understanding, I step forward on my healing journey, ready to redefine love and build a life filled with compassion, strength, and self-empowerment.

Meditative Healing Thought of the Day

In the stillness of my heart, I embrace the truth that I cannot change my father's behavior. This realization allows me to release the burden of holding onto expectations that lead to disappointment. As I breathe in, I choose to exhale the weight of resentment, freeing my spirit to journey towards forgiveness.

I acknowledge that forgiveness isn't an endorsement of his actions but a path to my inner peace. With each mindful breath, I release the grip of control and surrender to the understanding that his choices are beyond my influence.

I let go of the past's grip on my emotions by grounding myself in the present moment. With every exhale, I release the need to change him and instead focus on changing my perspective. I choose to nurture compassion for both his humanity and my journey.

In this meditative space, I am embracing the power of acceptance. I allow forgiveness to blossom from a place of self-empowerment, recognizing that I am taking ownership of my emotional well-being by relinquishing my desire to control his actions.

As I continue to breathe, I release any expectations of him conforming to my wishes. Instead, I focus on the present and the transformative journey of forgiveness. With every breath, I grant myself permission to release the past's grip and embrace the freedom from accepting the unchangeable.

Deeper Connection Within

1. What emotions do I still carry from my past with my father?

_____

_____

_____

_____

_____

_____

2. How have these emotions impacted my well-being and choices?

_____

_____

_____

_____

_____

_____

3. What does healing mean to me in my relationship with my father?

_____

_____

_____

_____

_____

_____

Loving Statements About Me

I release the past and open my heart to forgiveness.

I choose to heal and let go of old wounds.

Forgiveness is a gift I give to myself for my peace.

Gratitude Reflection of the Day

Today, I am grateful for my father, a source of wisdom and guidance. I appreciate the lessons he has taught me and the love he has shared.

Inner Reflections

I Forgive You For Abandoning Our Relationship

Forgiveness Inner Reflection of the Day

Navigating the path of healing and forgiveness regarding my father's abandonment has been a profound inner journey. Confronting the pain of being abandoned when I needed him most has brought me face to face with a complex mix of emotions – anger, sadness, confusion, and even a sense of inadequacy. But in this reflection, I seek to unravel the threads of forgiveness.

I acknowledge that his abandonment wasn't a reflection of my worth but his struggles and limitations. While his actions left scars, I'm now exploring the possibility of healing those wounds by extending forgiveness. It's not about condoning his actions but about releasing myself from resentment and bitterness.

This process has taught me that forgiveness isn't linear. It's okay to feel anger and sadness while working towards forgiveness. I permit myself to grieve the loss I experienced and the pain I endured. Through compassion, I'm finding a way to heal my own heart.

Forgiving my father is not solely about him but about my well-being. As I open myself to forgiveness, I am acknowledging my strength. Forgiveness doesn't excuse his actions, but it sets me free from carrying the weight of those actions.

In this inner reflection, I contemplate the possibility of empathy. I try to understand what might have driven him to choose – his challenges, fears, and circumstances. This doesn't make his actions right but helps humanize his decisions.

As I tread the path of forgiveness, I'm paving the way for my healing. I envision a future where the wounds of abandonment no longer define me. I am reclaiming my power and refusing to let his actions control my emotional landscape.

Through this inner journey, I am learning that forgiveness is a process and that taking my time is okay. By acknowledging my feelings, seeking understanding, and embracing self-compassion, I am forging a path toward healing, liberation, and a future where his abandonment does not define me.

Meditative Healing Thought of the Day

In the gentle embrace of mindfulness, I opened my heart to the understanding that my father parented me through his pain. As I breathe in, I absorb that his actions were shaped by his experiences, limitations, and struggles. With each exhale, I release judgment and make room for forgiveness.

In this meditative moment, I acknowledge that his wounds and challenges influenced his best. As I let go of resentment, I invite compassion to flow through me. Through understanding, I recognize that his actions were not an intentional infliction but a response to his journey.

With every mindful breath, I offer myself the grace of empathy. I release the weight of blame and choose to see his humanity. As I exhale, I remove the expectation of perfection and embrace the imperfections that shaped us.

By focusing on the present moment, I free myself from the grip of the past's pain. I choose to embrace forgiveness as a healing balm for my heart. As I continued to breathe, I let go of his need for validation, finding strength in granting validation to myself.

In this meditation, I create space for forgiveness to flourish. I acknowledge that his actions were intertwined with his struggles, and I release the desire to change his past choices. I honor my journey with each breath and extend my understanding to him.

Deeper Connection Within

1. Can I identify any patterns in my interactions with him that need healing?

_____

_____

_____

_____

_____

_____

2. What aspects of forgiveness feel challenging or liberating to me?

_____

_____

_____

_____

_____

_____

3. How can I create a safe space to process and heal from these emotions?

_____

_____

_____

_____

_____

_____

Loving Statements to About Me.

I am free from the burden of resentment.

Healing is a journey, and I embrace it with patience and grace.

I am worthy of healing and moving forward with a light heart.

Gratitude Reflection of the Day

I'm thankful for the moments of connection and understanding we've shared, reminding me of the importance of cherishing our relationship.

Inner Reflections

I Forgive You For The Lack Of Positive Affirmations

Forgiveness Inner Reflection of the Day

Reflecting on my memories, I acknowledge the absence of positive words and nurturing gestures from my father. This realization brings forth a mix of emotions – sadness, longing, and a deep sense of unmet needs. As I delve into forgiveness, I am confronted with the opportunity to release these lingering emotions and move beyond the shadows of the past.

In this inner reflection, I am learning to detach my sense of self-worth from his words and actions. His inability to provide the nurturing and positivity I craved does not define my value. His limitations might have resulted from his struggles and upbringing.

I choose to view forgiveness as an act of self-liberation. By forgiving, I am no longer tethered to the negativity and lack I experienced. It doesn't mean that I'm excusing his behavior; instead, I'm breaking free from the emotional grip it had on me.

Through forgiveness, I am learning to provide myself with the nurturing and positive reinforcement I longed for. I am cultivating self-compassion, embracing the truth that I can validate my worth and offer myself the love I deserve.

This reflection has taught me that healing requires a conscious decision to release the past. While I can't change my father's actions, I can change my response. I am choosing to replace resentment with empathy and to transform hurt into empowerment.

I am reframing my narrative. Instead of dwelling on what was missing, I am focusing on what I can cultivate within myself. I can nurture my growth, foster self-love, and become the cheerful voice guiding me.

As I embrace forgiveness, I am stepping into a future unburdened by the weight of memories. I am creating space for positivity, self-empowerment, and a newfound belief in my worth. Forgiveness is my path to liberation, where I choose to rise above the shadows of the past and define my narrative of healing and growth.

Meditative Healing Thought of the Day

In the tranquil realm of mindfulness, I realize that even if my father had showered me with more positive accolades, it wouldn't have fundamentally changed who I am. As I inhale, I let go of the yearning for external validation, understanding that my worth lies within. With each exhale, I release the grip of disappointment and allow forgiveness to bloom.

I acknowledge that his words, while impactful, wouldn't have shaped the essence of my being. By embracing this truth, I relinquish the hold of seeking validation from him. As I exhale, I invite self-acceptance and self-love to flourish.

In this meditative journey, I recognize that my worth isn't dependent on his accolades. With each mindful breath, I celebrate my uniqueness and intrinsic value. I release the weight of expectation and open my heart to forgiveness, freeing myself from validation-seeking.

As I continue to breathe, I let go of the past's grip and empower myself to define my worth. I honor my journey and the strength I've cultivated through self-discovery. With every inhale and exhale, I invite forgiveness as a liberating force that empowers me to validate myself.

In this moment of mindfulness, I redirect my focus from external validation to internal self-worth. I acknowledge that his words couldn't define my essence. Through forgiveness, I embrace the power to recognize my values, regardless of accolades or their absence.

Deeper Connection Within

1. What self-care practices can I incorporate to support my healing journey?

_____

_____

_____

_____

_____

_____

2. What beliefs about myself were shaped by my past with my father, and how can I shift them positively?

_____

_____

_____

_____

_____

_____

3. How can I empathize with my father's struggles and limitations?

_____

_____

_____

_____

_____

_____

Loving Statements About Me

Forgiveness liberates me from the chains of the past.

I release the pain and invite healing into my heart.

I choose to focus on my growth and well-being.

Gratitude Reflection of the Day

I appreciate the times when we've found common ground and discovered new ways to bond, deepening our connection and creating cherished memories.

Inner Reflections

I Welcome Forgiveness Energy As I Heal From Your Absence In My Life

Forgiveness Inner Reflection of the Day

Reflecting on my father's absence, I recognize its impact on my relationships with men. The void left by his absence has sometimes led to uncertainty about healthy boundaries and a hesitancy to welcome positive energy. As I embark on a journey of forgiveness, I also embrace the opportunity to redefine my interactions and create healthier dynamics.

In this reflection, I acknowledge that my father's absence does not determine my worth or ability to foster healthy connections. I understand that his choices were his own, and they do not dictate the outcomes of my relationships. Forgiveness allows me to separate his actions from my journey.

I am learning to set boundaries that honor my needs and well-being. I recognize that boundaries are not barriers but safeguards that ensure my emotional health and self-respect. By welcoming positive energy and establishing boundaries, I am creating a space where I can engage with men from a place of empowerment.

Through forgiveness, I release the weight of the past that may have influenced my interactions. I am no longer defined solely by his absence; my capacity for growth and resilience defines me. Forgiveness empowers me to reshape my narrative and move forward without the burden of resentment.

As I navigate this inner reflection, I embrace the possibility of forming connections based on mutual respect, trust, and understanding. I am allowing myself to heal and learn from my experiences, opening the door to authentic and positive relationships with men who align with my values.

Forgiveness allows me to create a new story where I control my interactions and emotions. I let go of the past, step into my power, and welcome positive energy while maintaining healthy boundaries. By forgiving my father and myself, I am reclaiming my ability to build relationships that nourish my soul and contribute to my growth.

Meditative Healing Thought of the Day

In the serenity of mindfulness, I acknowledge that my healing is not contingent upon receiving an apology from my father. As I inhale, I release the need for external validation or remorse. With each exhale, I create space for forgiveness to flow through me.

I recognize that my journey towards healing is within my control, independent of his actions. By embracing this truth, I let go of the expectation of an apology. As I exhale, I welcome self-empowerment and self-healing.

I honor my emotions without attaching them to his actions in this meditative moment. With each mindful breath, I grant myself permission to heal and thrive, regardless of external factors. I release the burden of waiting for an apology and invite forgiveness to take root.

As I breathe, I release the past's grip and focus on my present and future well-being. I acknowledge that I possess the strength to heal and grow, even without an apology. With every inhale and exhale, I invite forgiveness as a transformative force that empowers me to heal on my terms.

In this mindful reflection, I embrace the power of self-compassion and self-healing. I can move forward without being dependent on external validation. Through forgiveness, I create a path to my emotional liberation, irrespective of apologies.

Deeper Connection Within

1. How might his upbringing and experiences have influenced his actions?

_____

_____

_____

_____

_____

_____

2. What underlying pain behind his actions led to my wounds?

_____

_____

_____

_____

_____

_____

3. What aspects of his humanity and imperfections can I learn to understand?

_____

_____

_____

_____

_____

_____

Loving Statements About Me

My emotions are valid, and I honor them as part of my healing process.

I am resilient and can transform my emotions into strength.

Each day, I grow stronger in my journey of healing.

Gratitude Reflection of the Day

Today, I send thoughts of gratitude to my father, recognizing the sacrifices and love he has poured into our family.

Inner Reflections

_____
_____
_____
_____
_____
_____
_____
_____
_____
_____
_____
_____
_____
_____
_____
_____
_____
_____
_____
_____
_____
_____
_____
_____
_____
_____
_____
_____
_____
_____

I Forgive My Mind For Believing Your Personal Choices Ruined My Life

Forgiveness Inner Reflection of the Day

In my journey of forgiveness, I reflect on the belief that my father intentionally ruined my life. This thought has caused me pain and resentment, and it's time to release its grip on my well-being. My mind, seeking understanding, might have attributed intention to his actions. However, I am now shifting my perspective and practicing forgiveness towards my father and myself.

I recognize that holding onto the belief that he intentionally caused harm only perpetuates my suffering. By acknowledging the complexity of human behavior and motivations, I release the weight of this assumption. Forgiveness offers me a chance to reinterpret his actions as a reflection of his struggles rather than a deliberate attempt to hurt me.

In this reflection, I am learning to forgive my mind for grasping this belief. My mind seeks to make sense of experiences, even if it means assigning intention where it might not exist. Through forgiveness, I am granting myself the grace to let go of judgments and embrace a more compassionate understanding.

I am reframing my narrative by focusing on the lessons I've gained from challenges rather than dwelling on perceived intentions. I am empowering myself to transcend the limitations of bitterness and resentment. As I forgive my mind, I invite healing and growth to take its place.

By practicing forgiveness, I am not absolving his actions but liberating myself from the burden of assuming intent. I am fostering empathy and choosing to prioritize my emotional well-being. With this inner reflection, I am making space for healing, personal transformation, and a future unburdened by the weight of perceived intentions.

Meditative Healing Thought of the Day

In the gentle realm of mindfulness, I commit to releasing judgment of my father's decisions and shedding the cloak of victimhood I've worn. As I inhale, I let go of the weight of determination and victim mentality. With each exhale, I make space for forgiveness to permeate my being.

I acknowledge that his decisions, however flawed, were influenced by his experiences and challenges. By releasing judgment, I embrace the path of understanding and empathy. As I exhale, I welcome the transformation that forgiveness brings.

In this meditative space, I choose to relinquish the role of a victim and step into the power of resilience. With each mindful breath, I affirm my ability to overcome challenges and grow stronger. I release the grip of victimhood and invite self-empowerment.

As I continue to breathe, I let go of the past's grip on my identity. I focus on my present potential and future growth. With every inhale and exhale, I invite forgiveness as a catalyst for self-liberation from judgment and victim mentality.

In this mindful reflection, I embrace the power of choosing my response to his decisions. I acknowledge that I can transcend victimhood and forge a path of empowerment. Through forgiveness, I release the chains of judgment and step into the light of self-empowerment and understanding.

Deeper Connection Within

1. How can practicing empathy contribute to my healing and forgiveness?

_____

_____

_____

_____

_____

_____

2. How can I find common ground with my father despite our differences?

_____

_____

_____

_____

_____

_____

3. What experiences may have shaped his perspectives and behavior?

_____

_____

_____

_____

_____

_____

Loving Statements About Me

I am capable of replacing negative emotions with positive ones.

My heart is open to love and understanding, even in challenging situations.

I am creating a space within me for healing and positivity.

Gratitude Reflection of the Day

I'm grateful for the opportunities we've had to grow and learn from each other, fostering a sense of mutual respect and admiration.

Inner Reflections

DAY 6

I Forgive My Mind For Believing Work Was More Important Than Our Family

Forgiveness Inner Reflection of the Day

In the journey of forgiveness, I reflect upon the belief that my father's work was more important than our family. This belief has stirred emotions of neglect and hurt within me. As I explore forgiveness, I recognize that my mind might have oversimplified a complex situation. I am ready to release this belief and find understanding and healing.

I acknowledge that my father's choices regarding work were influenced by various factors – responsibilities, expectations, and even his upbringing. Through forgiveness, I can move beyond the confines of black-and-white thinking. I am embracing the possibility that his actions were not solely a reflection of value judgments but rather a response to many pressures.

Forgiveness prompts me to let go of the weight of resentment this belief has carried. I understand that my father's work choices were not intended to minimize the importance of our family. By releasing this belief, I can see a more nuanced picture.

As I navigate this inner reflection, I forgive my mind for holding onto this belief without considering the complexities of his circumstances. I recognize that my mind seeks explanations, often leading to oversimplification. Through forgiveness, I am fostering self-compassion and understanding.

I choose to reframe this belief. Instead of focusing on what I perceived as neglect, I am focusing on the times he was present, the lessons I've learned, and the strength I've gained from the challenges. Forgiveness allows me to transform my perspective from one of hurt to one of growth and resilience.

By forgiving my mind and releasing this belief, I am liberating myself from the grip of past assumptions. I am embracing the capacity for empathy and a deeper understanding of the complexity of human choices. With this inner reflection, I am making space for healing and allowing myself to move forward with an open heart and a willingness to let go of past judgments.

Meditative Healing Thought of the Day

In the serene realm of mindfulness, I accept my father's efforts to provide and his attempt to find a balance that aligns with his comfort. As I inhale, I release any expectations that he should have done things differently. With each exhale, I make room for forgiveness to flow through me.

I recognize that his sense of comfort and understanding drove his actions. By embracing this truth, I let go of the weight of unrealistic expectations. As I exhale, I invite empathy and compassion to fill the space within.

In this meditative moment, I acknowledge his efforts to provide and his attempt to navigate life in a way that felt right to him. With each mindful breath, I relinquish the need to impose my expectations on his actions. I invite understanding and forgiveness.

As I continue to breathe, I release the grip of past judgments and focus on the present acceptance of his choices. With every inhale and exhale, I welcome forgiveness as a healing force that allows me to release resentment and find peace.

I am embracing the power of understanding and empathy in this mindful reflection. I acknowledge that his comfort and experiences influenced his choices. Through forgiveness, I grant myself the freedom to release the grip of judgment and find solace in acceptance.

Deeper Connection Within

1. What does forgiveness mean to me, and how can it free me?

_____

_____

_____

_____

_____

_____

2. What expectations of apologies or acknowledgment am I willing to release?

_____

_____

_____

_____

_____

_____

3. How can letting go of resentment benefit my emotional well-being?

_____

_____

_____

_____

_____

_____

Loving Statements About Me

I nurture myself with compassion and self-care.

I am open to shifting my perspective and thoughts about my father.

I release judgment and choose to see him with empathy.

Gratitude Reflection of the Day

I appreciate the laughter and joy he brings into my life, reminding me of the importance of finding happiness in every season of our relationship.

Inner Reflections

I Forgive My Father For Choosing His Addiction Over Me

Forgiveness Inner Reflection of the Day

In my pursuit of healing and forgiveness, I reflect on the painful reality of a father who chose his addiction over me. This journey prompts me to explore the depths of my emotions – the hurt, the betrayal, and the abandonment I felt. As I navigate forgiveness, I reclaim my power to curate healing and growth after this profound experience.

I recognize that his choice was not a reflection of my worth but a manifestation of his struggles. Through forgiveness, I acknowledge the complexity of addiction and its grip on one's life. While his actions caused wounds, I chose to rise above the pain and find solace in my healing journey.

Forgiveness doesn't condone his actions; instead, it's a choice to release the emotional burden his choices placed on me. By forgiving, I am setting myself free from resentment and embracing the possibility of moving forward with resilience.

In this reflection, I forgive myself for any self-blame or feelings of inadequacy I may have carried. Addiction's impact on loved ones is complex, and I acknowledge that my feelings and reactions were valid responses to a difficult situation.

I am reframing my narrative. Instead of defining myself by his absence or addiction, I focus on the strength I've cultivated and the wisdom I've gained from overcoming adversity. Forgiveness is my way of choosing self-compassion over self-condemnation.

By practicing forgiveness, I am carving a path toward inner healing. I want to channel my energy into my growth, well-being, and ability to create a life that transcends the shadows of the past. Through this inner reflection, I am affirming my capacity to heal, thrive, and find peace despite the pain of his choices.

Meditative Healing Thought of the Day

In mindfulness, I embrace the truth that my father's addiction led him to make unhealthy decisions. As I inhale, I release the burden of blame and resentment. With each exhale, I create space for understanding and forgiveness to flow through me.

I acknowledge that addiction is a powerful force that can cloud judgment and distort decisions. By recognizing this truth, I let go of the weight of holding him solely responsible for his choices. As I exhale, I invite empathy and compassion into my heart.

In this meditative moment, I choose to separate his actions from his struggle with addiction. With each mindful breath, I release the need to judge him solely based on his decisions. I invite understanding and forgiveness to replace resentment.

As I continue to breathe, I release the grip of past anger and focus on the present path of healing and empathy. With every inhale and exhale, I invite forgiveness as a liberating force that allows me to untangle the complexities of addiction from the person he was.

In this mindful reflection, I am embracing the power of empathy and compassion. I acknowledge that addiction is a formidable challenge that affects decision-making. Through forgiveness, I free myself from the cycle of blame and resentment, creating space for understanding and healing to flourish.

Deeper Connection Within

1. What steps can I take to forgive my father, even if he doesn't change?

_____

_____

_____

_____

_____

_____

2. How would forgiving my father impact my growth and transformation?

_____

_____

_____

_____

_____

_____

3. What rituals or practices can I use to symbolize my intention to forgive?

_____

_____

_____

_____

_____

_____

Loving Statements About Me

I embrace forgiveness as a path to understanding and growth.

My heart is open to finding common ground with my father.

The past does not define me; I can shape my thoughts in the present.

Gratitude Reflection of the Day

I'm thankful for his unwavering support and encouragement, knowing that he is always there to lift me up in times of need.

Inner Reflections

I Forgive You For The Inconsistent Presence In My Life

Forgiveness Inner Reflection of the Day

As I embark on a journey of forgiveness, I reflect upon the inconsistent presence of my father in my life. This reflection unearths emotions – from disappointment to longing and even a sense of abandonment. However, I am learning to untangle these emotions and find a path towards healing and inner peace through forgiveness.

I recognize that his inconsistency resulted from his struggles and circumstances. Through forgiveness, I am embracing the understanding that his actions were not a reflection of my value but a manifestation of his limitations. By releasing the weight of resentment, I can move beyond the pain.

Forgiveness does not excuse his behavior; rather, it liberates me from the emotional burden of carrying his inconsistencies with me. I focus on my growth rather than remaining anchored in the past.

In this reflection, I am learning to forgive myself for any feelings of unworthiness that his inconsistency may have triggered. I acknowledge that my emotions are valid responses to a complex situation.

I am reframing my narrative. Instead of defining my sense of belonging by his presence, I am focusing on the strength I've developed from navigating his absence. Forgiveness allows me to transform pain into empowerment.

By practicing forgiveness, I am embracing the possibility of healing and growth. I am letting go of the notion that his actions determine my emotional well-being. Through this inner reflection, I am affirming my commitment to my healing journey and cultivating a sense of inner peace that transcends his inconsistent presence in my life.

Meditative Healing Thought of the Day

In mindfulness, I embrace the wisdom that forgiveness starts with my accountability for being present. As I inhale, I release the grip of dwelling in the past. With each exhale, I create space for personal empowerment and forgiveness to flow within me.

I acknowledge that I can shape my narrative by being present in the here and now. By recognizing this truth, I let go of the tendency to live in the shadows of the past. As I exhale, I invite self-empowerment and liberation from the chains of old wounds.

In this meditative moment, I step into my power and take charge of my present moment. With each mindful breath, I release the need to linger in the past's pain. I invite self-accountability and forgiveness to guide my journey forward.

As I continue to breathe, I release the grip of past regrets and focus on the potential of my present. With every inhale and exhale, I invite forgiveness as a transformative force that allows me to reclaim my agency and create a brighter future.

In this mindful reflection, I am embracing the power of being present in my own life. I acknowledge that my journey to forgiveness begins with my willingness to take ownership of my present. Through forgiveness, I am allowing myself to shed the weight of the past and walk the path of empowerment and growth.

Deeper Connection Within

1. What boundaries do I need to set in my current relationship with my father?

_____

_____

_____

_____

_____

_____

2. How can I communicate my boundaries effectively and respectfully?

_____

_____

_____

_____

_____

_____

3. What self-care practices can I adopt to maintain emotional balance while healing?

_____

_____

_____

_____

_____

_____

Loving Statements About Me

I am capable of cultivating empathy and compassion towards my father.

I focus on his humanity and imperfections, just like my own.

I release blame and allow space for understanding and healing.

Gratitude Reflection of the Day

Today, I send loving energy to my heart, acknowledging the love and appreciation I have for my father and the love he has for me.

Inner Reflections

I Forgive You For Not Accepting Help To Heal

Forgiveness Inner Reflection of the Day

In my quest for healing and forgiveness, I reflect on my father's refusal to accept help. This reflection evoked frustration and concern as I wished for his well-being. However, through forgiveness, I am learning to navigate the complexities of this situation and release the weight of resentment.

I acknowledge that his decision not to accept help stems from his struggles and fears. Through forgiveness, I am embracing the understanding that his actions are not a reflection of my ability to provide support but rather a reflection of his journey.

Forgiveness is not an endorsement of his choices; it's a pathway to release the emotional burden I've carried. By forgiving, I detach my well-being from his decisions, granting myself the freedom to move forward.

In this reflection, I forgive myself for any inadequacy or helplessness I may have experienced. I acknowledge that his choices are beyond my control, and my emotions are valid responses to a challenging situation.

I am reframing my narrative. Instead of holding onto resentment, I am focusing on the love and concern I've offered. Forgiveness empowers me to transform my frustration into compassion and to honor his autonomy.

By practicing forgiveness, I am nurturing my well-being and growth. I am letting go of the need to carry his choices as a personal responsibility. Through this inner reflection, I affirm my commitment to finding peace within myself, regardless of his decision to accept help.

Meditative Healing Thought of the Day

In mindfulness, I am intentionally releasing the habit of judging my father's choices for his life. As I inhale, I let go of the tendency to impose my values onto his journey. With each exhale, I create space for understanding and forgiveness to flow through me.

His experiences, circumstances, and perspective shaped my father's choices. By embracing this truth, I release the weight of judgment and open my heart to empathy. As I exhale, I invite compassion and forgiveness to fill my inner space.

In this meditative moment, I respect his autonomy to make choices that align with his path. With each mindful breath, I relinquish the need to label his decisions as right or wrong from my perspective. I invite acceptance and forgiveness.

As I continue to breathe, I release the grip of past judgments and focus on fostering understanding and connection. With every inhale and exhale, I invite forgiveness as a transformative force that helps me let go of the need to impose my judgments onto his journey.

In this mindful reflection, I am embracing the power of allowing individuals to make choices that resonate with their own lives. I acknowledge that my journey toward forgiveness involves letting go of the need to judge his decisions from my viewpoint. Through forgiveness, I am creating space for empathy and understanding to flourish.

Deeper Connection Within

1. How can I prioritize my well-being without feeling guilty?

_____

_____

_____

_____

_____

2. What boundaries can I establish to protect myself from future hurt?

_____

_____

_____

_____

_____

3. How can I find strength in upholding these boundaries, regardless of his response?

_____

_____

_____

_____

_____

_____

Loving Statements to About Me.

I am a channel of love and compassion towards myself and others.

Love is a powerful force that heals and transforms my heart.

I am capable of extending compassion to my father as I heal.

Gratitude Reflection of the Day

I'm grateful for the moments when we've chosen to communicate openly and honestly, strengthening our bond and creating a foundation of trust.

Inner Reflections

I Forgive You For The Decades Of Emotional Neglect

Forgiveness Inner Reflection of the Day

As I delve into the journey of forgiveness, I confront the profound impact of decades of emotional neglect by my father. This reflection brings forth emotions – from deep sadness to frustration and a sense of unmet needs. However, I am embracing the opportunity to heal, release, and transform these emotions through forgiveness.

I recognize that his emotional neglect was not a reflection of my worth but a manifestation of his limitations and struggles. Through forgiveness, I acknowledge the complexity of human relationships and how our own experiences can influence our actions.

Forgiveness is not a validation of his neglect; instead, it is an act of self-compassion. By releasing the grip of resentment, I am granting myself the freedom to move beyond the weight of unmet expectations.

In this reflection, I am learning to forgive myself for seeking validation and emotional nourishment from a source that could not provide it. I acknowledge that my feelings are valid responses to a challenging dynamic.

I am reframing my narrative. Instead of defining my emotional well-being by his neglect, I am focusing on the strength I've developed from overcoming this adversity. Forgiveness empowers me to transform pain into resilience and growth.

By practicing forgiveness, I am cultivating my emotional healing and well-being. I am letting go of the need for his validation and instead focusing on nurturing my self-worth. Through this inner reflection, I am affirming my commitment to finding peace within myself despite the emotional neglect I experienced.

Meditative Healing Thought of the Day

In mindfulness, I am intentionally releasing the weight of decades of emotional neglect from my relationship with my father. As I inhale, I gather the courage to let go of the accumulation of unmet emotional needs. With each exhale, I create space for healing and forgiveness to flow through me.

I recognize that carrying the burden of emotional neglect only perpetuates my suffering. By embracing this truth, I release the grip of resentment and make room for self-compassion. As I exhale, I invite healing and forgiveness to nurture my wounded heart.

In this meditative moment, I reclaim my emotional well-being by letting go of the past's grip. I release the attachment to unfulfilled expectations and yearnings with each mindful breath. I invite self-love and forgiveness into the depths of my being.

As I continue to breathe, I release the hold of past pain and focus on the potential for present healing. With every inhale and exhale, I invite forgiveness as a powerful agent of transformation that helps me release the shackles of emotional neglect and embrace a path of self-renewal.

In this mindful reflection, I am embracing the power of releasing emotional baggage. I acknowledge that carrying the weight of neglect hinders my growth. I am reclaiming my emotional well-being through forgiveness and offering myself the healing I deserve.

Deeper Connection Within

1. What positive qualities or traits can I identify in my father?

_____

_____

_____

_____

_____

_____

2. How can I reframe my memories to focus on moments of connection or growth?

_____

_____

_____

_____

_____

_____

3. What valuable life lessons have I learned from my experiences with my father?

_____

_____

_____

_____

_____

_____

Loving Statements to About Me.

Love and forgiveness go hand in hand, enriching my life.

I choose to break the cycle of negativity and embrace love.

Compassion is a strength that empowers me to heal and grow.

Gratitude Reflection of the Day

I appreciate the life lessons he has shared with me, helping me navigate the complexities of life with grace and resilience.

Inner Reflections

I Welcome Forgiveness Energy As I Heal From The Absence Of A Father's Love

Forgiveness Inner Reflection of the Day

As I embark on a path of forgiveness, I reflect on the absence of my father's love and its impact on my life. This reflection stirs emotions of longing, sadness, and even a sense of emptiness. Through forgiveness, I am navigating the complexity of these emotions and finding a way to release the pain they carry.

I acknowledge that his absence of love was not a reflection of my worthiness but a review of his struggles and limitations. Through forgiveness, I am granting myself the space to let go of the weight of unmet expectations and to move toward healing.

Forgiveness doesn't excuse his actions; instead, it's an act of compassion towards myself. By releasing resentment, I am allowing myself to create a new narrative not defined solely by his absence.

In this reflection, I forgive myself for seeking validation and love from a source that couldn't provide it. I recognize that my emotions are valid responses to a challenging situation.

I am reframing my narrative. Instead of focusing on what was lacking, I am focusing on the love and care I can offer myself. Forgiveness empowers me to transform pain into self-compassion and to cultivate my sense of worth.

By practicing forgiveness, I am fostering my emotional healing and growth. I am learning to let go of the need for external validation and instead nurturing my self-love. Through this inner reflection, I am affirming my commitment to finding peace within myself despite the absences I've experienced.

Meditative Healing Thought of the Day

In mindfulness, I am intentionally choosing to redefine gratitude for my father's unconventional love. As I inhale, I release the limitations of traditional expectations. With each exhale, I create space for a new perspective that transcends conventions and embraces uniqueness.

I recognize that gratitude doesn't have to conform to societal norms; it can be a profoundly personal and individual experience. By embracing this truth, I release the grip of comparison and open my heart to the beauty of diverse expressions of love. As I exhale, I invite acceptance and gratitude into my soul.

In this meditative moment, I honor my father's love for what it was rather than what it should have been. With each mindful breath, I release the constraints of judgment and open myself to the possibility of gratitude for his unique presence in my life. I invite understanding and forgiveness.

As I continue to breathe, I release the hold of past expectations and focus on the potential of present appreciation. With every inhale and exhale, I invite forgiveness as a transformative force that empowers me to redefine gratitude and embrace the unconventional aspects of love.

In this mindful reflection, I am embracing the power of rewriting my perspective on gratitude. I acknowledge that love takes many forms, and gratitude can be found in unconventional expressions. Through forgiveness, I am allowing myself to let go of preconceived notions and open my heart to the richness of diverse love experiences.

Deeper Connection Within

1. How can I use my journey with forgiveness to empower others or inspire change?

_____

_____

_____

_____

_____

_____

2. How might my story with my father contribute to my personal growth narrative?

_____

_____

_____

_____

_____

_____

3. What strengths have I developed due to the challenges I can embrace?

_____

_____

_____

_____

_____

_____

Loving Statements About Me

I am open to love, understanding, and harmony in my relationships.

I am capable of building bridges of love and empathy with my father.

I release the past and step into a future filled with positivity.

Gratitude Reflection of the Day

Today, I send kind and thankful thoughts to myself for being open to the growth and transformation that our relationship has offered.

Inner Reflections

I Forgive You For The Lack Of Active Listening

Forgiveness Inner Reflection of the Day

In my pursuit of forgiveness, I reflect on my father's lack of active listening and its impact on our relationship. This reflection surfaces emotions of frustration, invisibility, and a longing for genuine connection. Through forgiveness, I am navigating these emotions and seeking a way to release the weight they carry.

I recognize that his inability to listen actively reflected not my values but his communication patterns and challenges. By forgiving, I acknowledge the complexity of human interactions and how various factors can influence our behavior.

Forgiveness isn't an endorsement of his behavior; instead, it's a choice to liberate myself from the emotional burden of unmet expectations. I am allowing myself to move forward with a lighter heart by releasing resentment.

In this reflection, I forgive myself for seeking validation and understanding from someone who struggled to provide it. I understand that my feelings are valid responses to a challenging dynamic.

I am reframing my narrative. Instead of dwelling on his lack of active listening, I focus on my growth and communication skills. Forgiveness empowers me to transform frustration into patience and enhance my connection.

By practicing forgiveness, I am nurturing my emotional well-being and growth. I am letting go of the need for his validation and learning to communicate my needs effectively. Through this inner reflection, I affirm my commitment to finding peace within myself and fostering healthier interactions despite my challenges.

Meditative Healing Thought of the Day

In mindfulness, I intentionally reflect on the pattern of my expectations when my father listened and how his responses never seemed adequate. As I inhale, I release the grip of unmet expectations. With each exhale, I create space for understanding and forgiveness to flow within me.

I recognize that my quest for validation often overshadowed his efforts to engage. By embracing this truth, I release the weight of unfulfilled desires for validation. As I exhale, I invite empathy and compassion to fill my heart.

In this meditative moment, I choose to release the cycle of expecting more than his responses could provide. With each mindful breath, I relinquish the need for external validation and instead invite self-acceptance and self-love. I ask for understanding and forgiveness.

As I continue to breathe, I release the grip of past disappointments and focus on the potential of present acceptance. With every inhale and exhale, I invite forgiveness as a transformative force that helps me release the chains of expectation and embrace a path of self-validation.

In this mindful reflection, I am embracing the power of understanding the role my expectations played. I acknowledge that my journey towards forgiveness involves releasing the weight of unrealistic demands and embracing self-validation. I am creating space for empathy, understanding, and self-love to flourish through forgiveness.

Deeper Connection Within

1. How does my past with my father still affect my inner child's feelings and perceptions?

_____

_____

_____

_____

_____

_____

2. What actions can I take to nurture and heal my inner child's wounds?

_____

_____

_____

_____

_____

_____

3. How can I provide the love and support my inner child needs to feel safe?

_____

_____

_____

_____

_____

_____

Loving Statements to About Me.

With each breath, I release old pain and welcome renewal.

My heart is a space of renewal where healing blossoms.

I am open to the fresh opportunities that come with healing.

Gratitude Reflection of the Day

I'm thankful for the times when we've chosen forgiveness and understanding, allowing us to move forward with a sense of inner peace and hope.

Inner Reflections

I Forgive You For The Broken Promises

Forgiveness Inner Reflection of the Day

In my journey of forgiveness, I am reflecting on the broken promises made by my father and the impact they have left on my heart. This reflection stirs emotions of disappointment, mistrust, and a sense of letdown. Through forgiveness, I am navigating these emotions and discovering a way to release the weight they bear.

I recognize that his broken promises were not a reflection of my worth but a review of his struggles and limitations. Through forgiveness, I am embracing the understanding that life's complexities can lead to unfulfilled commitments. By releasing resentment, I am free to unburden my heart.

Forgiveness doesn't excuse his actions; instead, it's a choice to free myself from the emotional burden of unmet expectations. By forgiving, I can heal and move forward with a renewed sense of lightness.

In this reflection, I am forgiving myself for attaching hope and reliance to promises that were not fulfilled.

I understand my feelings are valid responses to a situation that hurt me.

I am reframing my narrative. Instead of fixating on the broken promises, I am focusing on my resilience and the lessons learned from navigating disappointment. Forgiveness empowers me to transform pain into growth and trust in my ability to overcome challenges.

By practicing forgiveness, I am nurturing my emotional healing and growth. I am letting go of the need for external validation and learning to rely on my strength. Through this inner reflection, I am affirming my commitment to finding peace within myself despite the broken promises I've experienced.

Meditative Healing Thought of the Day

In mindfulness, I intentionally reflect on the parallels between my broken promises and those my father didn't fulfill. As I inhale, I release the urge to judge him harshly, understanding that human imperfection is universal. With each exhale, I invite self-compassion and forgiveness to flow within me.

I acknowledge that I, too, need to catch up on promises and commitments. I release the weight of holding him to a higher standard by embracing this truth. As I exhale, I invite understanding and empathy into my heart.

In this meditative moment, I choose to break the cycle of judgment and extend the same grace to him that I wish for myself. With each mindful breath, I let go of resentment and invite forgiveness to permeate my being. I recognize that human frailty affects us all.

As I continue to breathe, I release the grip of past disappointments and focus on the potential for self-growth. With every inhale and exhale, I invite forgiveness as a transformative force that helps me release the burden of judgment and embrace the shared journey of making and breaking promises.

In this mindful reflection, I am embracing the power of recognizing my imperfections. I acknowledge that my journey towards forgiveness involves letting go of the need for perfection from others. Through forgiveness, I am creating space for understanding, empathy, and growth to flourish, both within me and in my relationship with my father.

Deeper Connection Within

1. What comforting practices can help me address and heal the wounds of my younger self?

_____

_____

_____

_____

_____

_____

2. How might my healing journey positively influence the healing of my inner child?

_____

_____

_____

_____

_____

_____

3. Can reconciliation with my father be possible, and what would it involve?

_____

_____

_____

_____

_____

_____

Loving Statements to About Me.

Every day, I am renewed as I let go of old wounds.

I embrace the power of renewal and growth within me.

I am worthy of a life free from the weight of the past.

Gratitude Reflection of the Day

I appreciate the moments of connection and shared laughter, reminding me of the beauty of our relationship.

Inner Reflections

I Forgive You For Prioritizing Others Over Me

Forgiveness Inner Reflection of the Day

In my pursuit of forgiveness, I reflect on when my father prioritized others over me and the emotions it stirred within me. This reflection evokes feelings of neglect, insignificance, and a longing for validation. Through forgiveness, I am learning to navigate these emotions and release the weight they carry.

I recognize that his choices to prioritize others reflected not my values but his relationships and responsibilities. Through forgiveness, I am embracing the understanding that many factors can influence people's actions. By releasing resentment, I am granting myself the freedom to heal from the wounds of perceived neglect.

Forgiveness doesn't justify his actions; instead, it's a choice to unburden myself from the emotional weight of comparison and unmet expectations. By forgiving, I am allowing myself to move forward without the chains of resentment.

In this reflection, I forgive myself for seeking validation and significance from external sources. I acknowledge that my feelings are valid responses to a complex dynamic that left me feeling overlooked.

I am reframing my narrative. Instead of dwelling on his choices to prioritize others, I focus on my growth and self-validation. Forgiveness empowers me to transform hurt into self-compassion and to recognize my worth regardless of external validation.

By practicing forgiveness, I am nurturing my emotional healing and growth. I am letting go of the need for others to prioritize me and embracing the power to validate myself. Through this inner reflection, I am affirming my commitment to finding peace within myself despite the times when I felt less prioritized.

Meditative Healing Thought of the Day

In mindfulness, I intentionally reflect on my father prioritizing to the best of his ability, even if some of his decisions inadvertently caused pain. As I inhale, I release the grip of judgment and open my heart to understanding his intentions. With each exhale, I invite compassion and forgiveness to flow within me.

I acknowledge that his decisions, however imperfect, were made based on his understanding of the circumstances. By embracing this truth, I release the weight of resentment and make room for empathy. As I exhale, I invite healing and reconciliation into my soul.

In this meditative moment, I honored his efforts to make the best choices, even if they led to unintended consequences. With each mindful breath, I release the need for blame and open myself to the possibility of forgiveness. I invite understanding and empathy.

As I continue to breathe, I release the grip of past pain and focus on the healing potential. With every inhale and exhale, I invite forgiveness as a transformative force that helps me let go of the need to judge his decisions and embrace the complexity of his journey.

I am embracing the power of recognizing his intentions in this mindful reflection. I acknowledge that my journey towards forgiveness involves letting go of the need for perfect decisions. Through forgiveness, I am creating space for understanding, empathy, and healing to flourish, both within me and in my relationship with my father.

Deeper Connection Within

1. How can I approach reconciliation with an open heart and clear intentions?

_____

_____

_____

_____

_____

_____

2. What fears or reservations do I have about reconnecting with my father?

_____

_____

_____

_____

_____

_____

3. How can I embrace forgiveness while keeping healthy expectations in reconciliation?

_____

_____

_____

_____

_____

_____

Loving Statements to About Me.

I release the old story and welcome a new chapter of healing.

I empower myself to rewrite my narrative with love and healing.

Healing is a gift I give myself, and I am worthy of it.

Gratitude Reflection of the Day

I'm grateful for his presence in my life, a constant source of support and love that fills my heart with warmth.

Inner Reflections

_____

_____

_____

_____

_____

_____

_____

_____

_____

_____

_____

_____

_____

_____

_____

_____

_____

_____

_____

_____

_____

_____

_____

_____

_____

_____

_____

_____

I Forgive You For The Empty Apologies

Forgiveness Inner Reflection of the Day

In my journey of forgiveness, I am reflecting on the empty apologies offered by my father and the emotions they have stirred within me. This reflection stirs frustration, disappointment, and a sense of unfulfilled reconciliation. Through forgiveness, I am navigating these emotions and seeking a way to release the weight they carry.

I recognize that his empty apologies were not a reflection of my worthiness of genuine amends but a manifestation of his difficulties in expressing remorse. I am acknowledging the complexity of human emotions and communication through forgiveness.

Forgiveness doesn't validate his insincere apologies but liberates me from the emotional burden of unmet expectations. By releasing resentment, I can heal from the hurt of unfulfilled reconciliations.

In this reflection, I forgive myself for seeking validation and closure from someone who struggled to provide it. I understand that my feelings are valid responses to a challenging dynamic.

I am reframing my narrative. Instead of focusing on his inability to apologize meaningfully, I am focusing on my capacity for emotional healing and growth. Forgiveness empowers me to transform frustration into self-compassion and understanding.

By practicing forgiveness, I am nurturing my well-being and resilience. I am letting go of the need for external validation and learning to validate my emotions. Through this inner reflection, I am affirming my commitment to finding peace despite the emptiness I've experienced in my apologies.

Meditative Healing Thought of the Day

In mindfulness, I am choosing to release the habit of judging how my father handled things and instead focus on seeing the good within him. As I inhale, I let go of the weight of criticism and negative perceptions. With each exhale, I create space for understanding and appreciation to bloom.

I recognize that his own experiences and perspective influenced his actions. By embracing this truth, I release the grip of judgment and open my heart to the possibility of finding positivity. As I exhale, I invite empathy and compassion into my thoughts.

In this meditative moment, I acknowledge his efforts and intentions, even if they may not align with my expectations. With each mindful breath, I relinquish the need to label his actions wrong and invite understanding and forgiveness to take their place. I choose to see his humanity and the good within him.

As I continue to breathe, I release the hold of past criticisms and focus on the potential for finding the positive in his journey. With every inhale and exhale, I invite forgiveness as a transformative force that helps me let go of judgment and see his actions through understanding and grace.

In this mindful reflection, I embrace the power of looking beyond judgment. I acknowledge that my journey toward forgiveness involves letting go of the need to criticize and embracing the capacity to see the good within him. Through forgiveness, I am creating space for empathy, understanding, and positivity to flourish in my perception of him.

Deeper Connection Within

1. What steps can I take to initiate a conversation or bridge the gap if I choose to?

_____

_____

_____

_____

_____

_____

2. In what ways have I grown understanding and more resilient due to my experiences?

_____

_____

_____

_____

_____

_____

3. How might my journey toward forgiveness empower me to live a more fulfilling life?

_____

_____

_____

_____

_____

_____

Loving Statements to About Me.

I am stronger than the wounds of the past; I am a survivor.

I discover strength and resilience as I heal and forgive.

Each step on this healing journey brings me closer to my true self.

Gratitude Reflection of the Day

Today, I am filled with gratitude for my father, the precious bond we share, and the hope for joy that resides in every season of our relationship.

Inner Reflections

I Welcome Forgiveness Energy As I Heal From The Rejection

Forgiveness Inner Reflection of the Day

In the depths of my healing journey, I confront the wounds inflicted by my father's rejection and abandonment. This reflection awakens emotions – from raw pain to a deep yearning for acceptance. Through forgiveness, I am navigating the labyrinth of these emotions and striving to free myself from their weight.

His rejection and abandonment did not indicate my value but reflected his struggles and choices. Forgiveness enables me to comprehend that his painful actions are not a definitive measure of my worth.

Forgiveness is not a validation of his choices; it's a choice to release the emotional burden they've placed upon me. By letting go of resentment, I can heal and reclaim my narrative.

This reflection allows me to forgive myself for internalizing his rejection and abandonment as reflections of my inadequacy. My feelings are valid responses to an immensely challenging situation.

I am rewriting my narrative. Instead of defining my self-worth by his actions, I focus on the resilience and growth I've gained from this experience. Forgiveness empowers me to convert pain into strength and self-compassion.

By embracing forgiveness, I am nurturing my emotional well-being and growth. I am relinquishing the need for his validation and recognizing my power to heal. Through this inner reflection, I reaffirm my commitment to find solace within myself, irrespective of the rejection and abandonment I've endured.

I welcome forgiveness energy as I heal from my father's rejection.

Meditative Healing Thought of the Day

In mindfulness, I intentionally accept that although I didn't cause the pain, I am responsible for embarking on the healing journey. As I inhale, I release the weight of blame and victimhood. With each exhale, I create space for empowerment and self-compassion to flourish.

I acknowledge that healing is personal, irrespective of who caused the pain. By embracing this truth, I release the grip of resentment and open my heart to the possibility of transformation. As I exhale, I invite self-healing and self-love into my thoughts.

In this meditative moment, I shifted my perspective from blame to empowerment. With each mindful breath, I release the need to assign responsibility for the pain and instead focus on my capacity to heal. I embrace the opportunity to remove the weight of the past.

As I continue to breathe, I release the hold of past wounds and focus on the potential for personal growth. With every inhale and exhale, I invite forgiveness as a transformative force that empowers me to take charge of my healing journey, regardless of who caused the pain.

In this mindful reflection, I am embracing the power of self-responsibility in the healing process. I acknowledge that my journey toward forgiveness involves releasing the need to place blame and embracing the power to heal and transform. Through forgiveness, I am creating space for empowerment, self-compassion, and growth to flourish within me.

Deeper Connection Within

1. How can I channel the strength gained from forgiveness into other areas of my life?

_____

_____

_____

_____

_____

_____

2. What new goals or dreams can I pursue now that I am healing and forgiving?

_____

_____

_____

_____

_____

_____

3. How can my journey inspire me to create positive change in my relationships and beyond?

_____

_____

_____

_____

_____

Loving Statements About Me

I am capable of embracing challenges with grace and empowerment.

My heart is a place of self-discovery and transformation.

I control my thoughts and emotions, guiding them towards healing.

Gratitude Reflection of the Day

I'm thankful for the opportunities we've had to create lasting memories and traditions, building a legacy of love and connection.

Inner Reflections

I Welcome Forgiveness' Healing Energy As I Accept...

Forgiveness Inner Reflection of the Day

As I journey toward forgiveness, I reflect on my relationship with my father and the understanding that he did his best despite his challenges. This contemplation brings forth emotions – from lingering disappointment to a glimmer of compassion. Through forgiveness, I am navigating these emotions and embracing the truth that his best effort, flawed as it may have been, was rooted in his limitations.

I acknowledge that his actions were not a reflection of my worth but rather an outcome of his circumstances and struggles. By practicing forgiveness, I am granting myself the freedom to detach from the weight of unmet expectations and move toward healing.

Forgiveness doesn't condone his choices; instead, it is an act of self-compassion. It allows me to release resentment and extend my understanding of human experiences' complexity.

In this reflection, I also forgive myself for seeking perfection in his actions and holding him to unrealistic standards. My feelings are valid responses to a complex relationship dynamic.

I am rewriting my narrative. Instead of dwelling on his imperfections, I focus on the strength and growth I've cultivated through this journey. Forgiveness empowers me to convert disappointment into empathy and to recognize the inherent humanity in us all.

By practicing forgiveness, I am nurturing my emotional well-being and personal growth. I am shedding the burden of blame and learning to offer grace to both him and myself. Through this inner reflection, I reaffirm my commitment to finding peace by acknowledging that he did his best given his circumstances.

I welcome forgiveness' healing energy as I accept you did your best.

Meditative Healing Thought of the Day

In mindfulness, I intentionally accept that "it" happened and cannot be changed. As I inhale, I release the burden of dwelling on the past. With each exhale, I create space for growth and transformation to unfold.

I recognize that dwelling on what happened only prolongs my suffering. By embracing this truth, I release the grip of resistance and open my heart to the possibility of personal growth. As I exhale, I invite self-empowerment and self-love into my thoughts.

In this meditative moment, I shift my focus from the past to the present and future possibilities. With each mindful breath, I release the attachment to what cannot be changed and invite the potential for growth and healing. I embrace the opportunity to become a better version of myself.

As I continue to breathe, I release the hold of past regrets and focus on the potential for personal evolution. With every inhale and exhale, I invite forgiveness as a transformative force that empowers me to redirect my energy from dwelling on the past to nurture my growth.

In this mindful reflection, I embrace the power of accepting what cannot be changed. I acknowledge that my journey towards forgiveness involves letting go of resistance and embracing the power to evolve. Through forgiveness, I am creating space for personal growth, self-empowerment, and transformation to flourish within me.

Deeper Connection Within

1. What lessons have my challenges with my father taught me, and how can I be grateful for them?

_____

_____

_____

_____

_____

_____

2. How can I find gratitude for the person my father has been, regardless of the pain?

_____

_____

_____

_____

_____

_____

3. How can acceptance of his imperfections and my own contribute to my healing?

_____

_____

_____

_____

_____

_____

Loving Statements About Me

I am grateful for the opportunity to heal and forgive.

Gratitude fills my heart as I release old wounds and embrace healing.

Each day is a new chance for growth and positivity.

Gratitude Reflection of the Day

I appreciate the strength and resilience we've shown in times of challenge, reminding me of the power of our family ties.

Inner Reflections

I Forgive My Mind For Believing I Wasn't Enough

Forgiveness Inner Reflection of the Day

In my pursuit of healing, I confront the deep-seated belief that I wasn't enough due to my father's abandonment. This reflection stirs emotions – from lingering inadequacy to a longing for validation. Through forgiveness, I am journeying through these emotions, reclaiming my self-worth, and freeing myself from the chains of this detrimental belief.

I acknowledge that his abandonment was not a reflection of my inherent worthiness but rather a reflection of his choices and circumstances. Forgiveness enables me to untangle my self-esteem from the web of his actions and preferences.

Forgiveness doesn't absolve his abandonment; it's an act of self-compassion. It allows me to release my emotional weight and embrace a new narrative that empowers me.

In this reflection, I forgive myself for internalizing his abandonment as proof of my inadequacy. My feelings are valid responses to a profoundly painful experience.

I am reframing my narrative. Instead of measuring my value by his presence or absence, I am focusing on the resilience and self-growth that have emerged from this journey. Forgiveness empowers me to transform feelings of unworthiness into self-love and acceptance.

By practicing forgiveness, I am nurturing my emotional healing and growth. I am relinquishing the grip of this belief that has held me captive for so long. Through this inner reflection, I am reaffirming my commitment to finding peace within myself, regardless of the past, and acknowledging that my worthiness is not contingent on the actions of others.

Meditative Healing Thought of the Day

In the realm of mindfulness, I am intentionally choosing to embrace the profound truth that I am enough, irrespective of my father's actions or choices. As I inhale, I release any doubts about my worthiness. With each exhale, I create space for self-acceptance and self-love to flourish.

I recognize that my worthiness isn't determined by external factors, including my father's behavior. By embracing this truth, I release the grip of seeking validation from others and open my heart to the certainty of my inherent value. As I exhale, I invite self-assurance and self-worth into my thoughts.

In this meditative moment, I affirm that I am enough exactly as I am. With each mindful breath, I release the need for validation from my father or anyone else. I invite self-love and self-acceptance to flow through me, guiding my journey.

As I continue to breathe, I release the hold of past insecurities and focus on the potential for unshakable self-belief. With every inhale and exhale, I invite forgiveness as a transformative force that empowers me to release the weight of seeking approval and to stand in my worthiness.

In this mindful reflection, I embrace the power of recognizing my enoughness. I acknowledge that my journey towards forgiveness involves letting go of the need for external validation and embracing the truth that I am inherently valuable. Through forgiveness, I am creating space for self-assurance, self-love, and self-acceptance to flourish within me.

Deeper Connection Within

1. What practices can I incorporate to remind myself to focus on gratitude and acceptance?

_____

_____

_____

_____

_____

_____

2. How can gratitude shape my perspective as I continue to heal?

_____

_____

_____

_____

_____

_____

3. How does my commitment to healing and forgiveness align with my vision for the future?

_____

_____

_____

_____

_____

_____

Loving Statements to About Me.

I am grateful for the lessons that pain has taught me.

Gratitude transforms my perception, guiding me toward healing.

I focus on the blessings in my life, fostering a positive mindset.

Gratitude Reflection of the Day

I'm thankful for the love that flows between us, creating a deep and unbreakable connection that I cherish.

Inner Reflections

DAY 19

I Forgive You For Not Seeing
The Greatness In Me

Forgiveness Inner Reflection of the Day

As I embark on a journey of forgiveness, I reflect on the profound impact of my father not seeing the greatness within me. This introspection awakens feelings of validation seeking, self-doubt, and unfulfilled longing. I am navigating these emotions through forgiveness, seeking to release their weight and rediscovering my self-worth.

My father's inability to recognize my greatness does not define my value. Through forgiveness, I acknowledge that his experiences and beliefs limit his perception. I am granting myself the freedom to embrace my self-perception by releasing resentment.

Forgiveness does not endorse his lack of recognition; instead, it is a choice to liberate myself from the emotional burden of seeking external validation. By practicing forgiveness, I am taking a step towards empowering myself.

In this reflection, I forgive myself for seeking approval and validation from someone unable to provide it. I

179

acknowledge that my feelings are valid responses to a profoundly human desire for acknowledgment.

I am rewriting my narrative. Instead of defining my worth by his perception, I focus on cultivating self-appreciation and self-awareness. Forgiveness empowers me to transform the need for external validation into the ability to celebrate my achievements.

By practicing forgiveness, I am nurturing my emotional well-being and growth. I am relinquishing the hold of seeking validation from others and learning to validate myself. Through this inner reflection, I am reaffirming my commitment to finding peace within myself and recognizing the greatness within me, irrespective of external recognition.

Meditative Healing Thought of the Day

In my journey toward forgiveness, I am reflecting on the pain caused by my father's consistent failure to show up in my life. This introspection stirs emotions of abandonment, disappointment, and a sense of yearning for a presence that was never fulfilled. Through forgiveness, I am navigating these emotions, seeking to release the burden they carry and forging a path toward healing.

I recognize that his absence was not a reflection of my worth but a manifestation of his struggles and choices. Through forgiveness, I am embracing the understanding that his actions resulted from his circumstances and limitations. By releasing resentment, I am granting myself the freedom to heal from the wounds of unmet expectations.

Forgiveness does not validate his absence; it's a choice to free myself from the emotional weight of longing for a presence that was never provided. By practicing forgiveness, I choose my emotional well-being over carrying the weight of past disappointments.

In this reflection, I forgive myself for seeking affirmation and attachment from someone who consistently let me down. My feelings are valid responses to a complex dynamic that isolated me.

I am reframing my narrative. Instead of focusing on his absence, I focus on the strength and resilience I've cultivated through this experience. Forgiveness empowers me to transform hurt into self-empowerment and recognize my healing capacity.

By practicing forgiveness, I am nurturing my emotional healing and personal growth. I am letting go of the need for external validation and choosing to validate my own experiences. Through this inner reflection, I am reaffirming my commitment to finding peace within myself, regardless of the absence I've endured.

Deeper Connection Within

1. How can I ensure my past wounds do not define my future?

_____

_____

_____

_____

_____

_____

2. How can I create a life where my father's actions have less influence over my happiness?

_____

_____

_____

_____

_____

_____

3. What kind of relationships do I want to cultivate moving forward?

_____

_____

_____

_____

_____

_____

Loving Statements About Me

I am thankful for the strength within me to overcome past wounds.

I welcome positivity and light into my heart as I heal.

I am open to change and transformation as I heal and forgive.

Gratitude Reflection of the Day

Today, I send thoughts of gratitude for the laughter and happiness that my father brings into my life, brightening even the darkest days.

Inner Reflections

I Forgive You For Not Showing Up

Forgiveness Inner Reflection of the Day

In my journey toward forgiveness, I am reflecting on the pain caused by my father's consistent failure to show up in my life. This introspection stirs emotions of abandonment, disappointment, and a sense of yearning for a presence that was never fulfilled. Through forgiveness, I am navigating these emotions, seeking to release the burden they carry and forging a path toward healing.

I recognize that his absence was not a reflection of my worth but a manifestation of his struggles and choices. Through forgiveness, I am embracing the understanding that his actions resulted from his circumstances and limitations. By releasing resentment, I am granting myself the freedom to heal from the wounds of unmet expectations.

Forgiveness does not validate his absence; it's a choice to free myself from the emotional weight of longing for a presence that was never provided. By practicing forgiveness, I choose my emotional well-being over carrying the weight of past disappointments.

In this reflection, I forgive myself for seeking affirmation and attachment from someone who consistently let me down. My feelings are valid responses to a complex dynamic that isolated me.

I am reframing my narrative. Instead of focusing on his absence, I focus on the strength and resilience I've cultivated through this experience. Forgiveness empowers me to transform hurt into self-empowerment and recognize my healing capacity.

By practicing forgiveness, I am nurturing my emotional healing and personal growth. I am letting go of the need for external validation and choosing to validate my own experiences. Through this inner reflection, I am reaffirming my commitment to finding peace within myself, regardless of the absence I've endured.

Meditative Healing Thought of the Day

In mindfulness, I intentionally shift my focus from blaming my father to recognizing the greatness within myself. As I inhale, I release the grip of resentment and blame. With each exhale, I create space for self-empowerment and self-recognition to blossom.

I recognize that dwelling on blame only hinders my growth. By embracing this truth, I release the weight of holding onto resentment and open my heart to the potential for self-discovery and self-appreciation. As I exhale, I invite self-love and self-empowerment into my thoughts.

In this meditative moment, I acknowledge the greatness within me, regardless of external circumstances. With each mindful breath, I release the need to place blame and invite self-recognition to guide my perspective. I embrace the opportunity to rise above blame and see my potential.

As I continue to breathe, I release the hold of past resentment and focus on the potential for personal growth. With every inhale and exhale, I invite forgiveness as a transformative force that empowers me to let go of blame and focus on nurturing my greatness.

In this mindful reflection, I am embracing the power of self-recognition. I acknowledge that my journey toward forgiveness involves releasing the grip of blame and embracing the greatness within me. Through forgiveness, I am creating space for self-empowerment, self-love, and personal growth to thrive within me.

Deeper Connection Within

1. How can I channel the energy of forgiveness into a future filled with freedom and peace?

_____

_____

_____

_____

_____

_____

2. How can I show myself compassion as I navigate the complexities of forgiveness?

_____

_____

_____

_____

_____

_____

3. What self-compassionate thoughts can I offer myself during moments of struggle?

_____

_____

_____

_____

_____

_____

Loving Statements About Me

I embrace the process of transformation with patience and courage.

Each day, I become a stronger and more empowered version of myself.

Change is a natural part of life; I welcome it with open arms.

Gratitude Reflection of the Day

I'm grateful for the moments of growth and self-discovery that our relationship has offered, reminding me of the importance of embracing change.

Inner Reflections

I Forgive My Mind For Believing You Are The Cause Of My Struggles With Men

Forgiveness Inner Reflection of the Day

In my pursuit of forgiveness, I am turning inward to reflect on how my mind has blamed my father for my romantic struggles. This introspection unveils emotions – from resentment to a sense of victimhood. Through forgiveness, I am navigating these emotions, releasing their grip, and freeing myself from the weight of this association.

I recognize that attributing my romantic struggles to my father is not a fair reflection of reality. By practicing forgiveness, I am acknowledging that my father's actions and my romantic experiences are separate entities. I am granting myself the freedom to reclaim my agency in matters of the heart.

Forgiveness isn't an endorsement of my father's actions; it's a choice to unburden myself from the emotional weight of blame. I am embracing the potential to shape my romantic narrative by releasing resentment.

In this reflection, I forgive myself for seeking an external scapegoat for my challenges. My feelings are valid responses to a desire to make sense of my experiences.

I am rewriting my narrative. Instead of assigning blame, I am focusing on owning my romantic journey. Forgiveness empowers me to transform blame into self-awareness and to recognize that my past does not dictate my present or future.

By practicing forgiveness, I am nurturing my emotional well-being and personal growth. I am shedding the need for external factors to define my romantic experiences. Through this inner reflection, I am reaffirming my commitment to finding peace within myself, releasing blame, and embracing the potential to create my own love story.

Meditative Healing Thought of the Day

In this meditative thought of the future, I envision a profound transformation within me. It's a future where I have forgiven my mind for believing that others cause my struggles with men. In this empowered future, I am the captain of my emotional ship, steering it towards calmer waters.

I see a version of myself who has unraveled the complex web of blame and resentment. I no longer believe that external factors define my happiness or my struggles. Instead, I recognize that my inner world, thoughts, and choices are the true architects of my experiences.

In this future, I stand tall and confident, knowing that I am not a victim of circumstances or the actions of others. I've taken responsibility for my own life and happiness. I've embraced the power of self-love and self-acceptance, realizing that I am complete and whole.

My relationships with men have transformed as well. I attract and nurture connections built on mutual respect, understanding, and support. I no longer seek validation or fulfillment from others but rather share my life with those who enhance it positively and meaningfully.

I am resilient and emotionally mature, able to communicate my needs and boundaries with clarity and compassion. I've learned that forgiveness is not a sign of weakness but a testament to my strength.

Forgiving my past grievances allows me to release the heavy burdens that held me back.

In this empowered future, I radiate love and positivity, not just in my relationships with men but in all aspects of my life. I've harnessed the energy once spent on blame and resentment to create a fulfilling and purposeful existence.

Meditating on this future, I feel a profound sense of liberation and joy. It is a future where I am the master of my destiny, have forgiven my mind for its past beliefs, and have embraced a life filled with love, resilience, and inner peace. This future is within my grasp, and I am ready to step into it with open arms and a heart full of empowerment.

Deeper Connection Within

1. How can my journey towards forgiving my father transform my relationship with myself?

_____

_____

_____

_____

_____

_____

2. What affirmations or mantras can remind me of my capacity for self-compassion?

_____

_____

_____

_____

_____

_____

3. How might practicing self-compassion accelerate my healing and transformation process?

_____

_____

_____

_____

_____

_____

Loving Statements About Me

I am a work in progress, constantly evolving towards healing and growth.

Transformation is my birthright, and I embrace it wholeheartedly.

I am open to the beautiful changes that come from forgiveness and healing.

Gratitude Reflection of the Day

I appreciate the enduring love and hope that we share, knowing that no matter the season, our bond remains a source of joy and fulfillment.

Inner Reflections

_____
_____
_____
_____
_____
_____
_____
_____
_____
_____
_____
_____
_____
_____
_____
_____
_____
_____
_____
_____
_____
_____
_____
_____
_____

BONUS

I Forgive My Father For "Protecting Me" By Lying to Me

Forgiveness Inner Reflection of the Day

Today, I contemplate the profound peace and inner joy that will blossom within me once I fully embrace forgiveness towards my father. The weight of his lies has burdened my heart for far too long, but I am now on a transformative journey towards release. As I navigate this path, I envision a future where the shackles of resentment no longer bind me.

In forgiving my father, I am not condoning his actions, but I am reclaiming my own inner peace. I recognize that his lies stemmed from his own fears and limitations, and I choose to set myself free from their grip.

With each step towards forgiveness, I feel the heavy burden lifting, making room for a profound sense of calm and tranquility. The inner joy that emerges is a testament to my strength and resilience.

As I look forward to the day when forgiveness is complete, I see a life filled with harmony and serenity. The past no longer holds me captive, and I am free to embrace the beauty of the present moment.

Today, I nurture the seeds of forgiveness within me, knowing that they will eventually blossom into a garden of peace and inner joy. I am on a path of healing, and I am filled with hope for the bright future that awaits me once I forgive my father and find true serenity within.

Meditative Healing Thought of the Day

As I journey toward forgiveness, I embrace the profound transformation that awaits me. In forgiving my father, I open the door to inner peace—a tranquil sanctuary where love and understanding flourish. Acknowledging the hurt he caused is the first step towards healing, and I am empowered by my capacity to love him despite the pain. With each passing moment, I am one step closer to a heart unburdened by resentment, and in that space, I find the serenity I've longed for.

Today, I walk the path of forgiveness, guided by the light of love and healing, and I am one step closer to the inner peace I deserve.

Deeper Connection Within

What do I need to tell myself the truth about?

_____
_____
_____
_____
_____
_____

What do I need to forgive myself for?

_____
_____
_____
_____
_____
_____

What actions can I take to heal?

_____
_____
_____
_____
_____
_____

Loving Statements About Me

I choose to embrace forgiveness and love in my heart for my father. With each passing day, my capacity for understanding and compassion grows, allowing me to release any lingering resentment and replace it with kindness.

I am open to healing and nurturing a loving relationship with my father. My thoughts are filled with empathy and empathy, and I am committed to fostering harmony and connection between us.

I affirm that I am capable of forgiving and loving my father unconditionally. I release any judgments or negative thoughts, and I embrace a mindset of compassion, recognizing the beauty of our shared journey.

Gratitude Reflection of the Day

Today, I am profoundly grateful for my father, a beacon of love, wisdom, and support in my life. I appreciate the deep connection we share, which has grown and evolved through the seasons of our relationship. Our journey together has taught me the value of forgiveness, understanding, and the enduring power of love. I'm thankful for his unwavering presence, always offering a listening ear and a warm heart.

I appreciate the moments of laughter and joy that we've shared, creating cherished memories that I hold close to my heart. Through the ups and downs, our bond has remained a source of inner peace and hope, reminding me of the beauty of familial love.

Today, I send thoughts of gratitude to my father, recognizing the profound impact he has had on my life and the love he continues to pour into our relationship. I am filled with thankfulness and appreciation for the seasons we've weathered together, and I look forward to the joy each new season will bring to our connection.

Inner Reflections

_____
_____
_____
_____
_____
_____
_____
_____
_____
_____
_____
_____
_____
_____
_____
_____
_____
_____
_____
_____
_____
_____
_____
_____
_____

Healing And Self-Empowerment

As the final pages of this journal are turned, a chapter of profound transformation ends. The journey you embarked upon, one of forgiveness, healing, and personal growth, has led you through the corridors of your heart, illuminated the corners of your soul, and guided you toward self-empowerment. It is a journey that has redefined your relationship with your father and, more importantly, your relationship with yourself.

In these pages, you have navigated the complexities of forgiveness—a journey that often demands courage, vulnerability, and the willingness to release the chains of resentment. Through introspection and introspective writing, you've explored the depths of your emotions, confronting the pain and hurt that have lingered from the past. You've learned that forgiveness is not about condoning hurtful actions but about liberating yourself from the weight of blame and bitterness. It is an act of reclaiming your power, choosing healing over suffering.

Embracing Healing

Healing is not a destination but an ongoing process that unfolds gradually and uniquely for each individual. Throughout this 21-day journal, you've embarked on a profound exploration of self-discovery, forgiveness, and self-compassion.

Patience and self-compassion have been your steadfast companions on this journey. You've nurtured your wounds with tenderness, acknowledging the pain and trauma of the past. You've taken significant steps toward wholeness and emotional liberation by tending to these scars and mending the broken pieces of your heart.

Mindful practices have been your guiding light, creating a safe and compassionate space to grieve, release, and transform. Through journaling, meditation, and self-reflection, you've cultivated a deep understanding of yourself and the patterns that may have influenced your life.

Your commitment to healing is a testament to your strength and resilience. It has enabled you to move beyond the confines of old wounds and embrace the vast realm of possibility. As you continue this journey, remember that healing is a process that unfolds in time. Be gentle with yourself, and allow the transformation to occur naturally.

Your story of healing is still being written, and it's a story of empowerment, growth, and self-discovery. Keep nurturing your inner world, continue to explore the depths of your emotions, and embrace the healing journey with an open heart. You can create a future filled with emotional liberation, self-compassion, and a profound sense of well-being.

Healing is a journey that requires patience and self-compassion. Throughout this journal, you've taken the steps to nurture your wounds, to tend to the scars of the past, and to mend the broken pieces of your heart. Through mindful practices, you've created a space of compassion and understanding where you've allowed yourself to grieve, release, and transform. Your commitment to healing has paved the way for growth, enabling you to move beyond the confines of old wounds and into the realm of possibility.

Taking Accountability

Taking accountability for your life is a profound and transformative shift, and I encourage you to continue embracing this empowering perspective. It marks a pivotal moment when you recognize your immense power in shaping your present and future.

In this journey, you've acknowledged that while you cannot alter the past, you have the agency to decide how you respond to it. You've reclaimed ownership over your choices, actions, and reactions by releasing blame and resentment. This powerful act of self-responsibility is a testament to your strength and resilience.

You've declared that you refuse to be defined by yesterday's wounds. Instead, you're forging a path to emotional liberation and personal growth. By taking accountability, you've harnessed the power to transcend the limitations of old narratives and create a narrative that aligns with your values and aspirations.

This transformation isn't just about acknowledging mistakes; it's about embracing the full spectrum of your humanity. It's about recognizing that you are not defined by your past but by your willingness to learn, grow, and evolve. It's a testament to your capacity to heal and thrive.

As you move forward, remember that accountability is a dynamic process. Be patient with yourself and continue to nurture your self-awareness. Your journey of taking accountability is ongoing, and each step brings you closer to a life defined by self-empowerment, authenticity, and emotional freedom. You've shown incredible courage by choosing this path, and I encourage you to keep walking it with unwavering determination and self-compassion.

A profound shift occurred when you chose to take accountability for your life. You recognized that while you cannot change the past, you hold the power to shape your present and future. By releasing blame, you've reclaimed agency over your choices, actions, and responses. This transformation is a testament to your strength and resilience—a declaration that you refuse to be defined by yesterday's wounds.

A New Perspective

As you close this chapter, you do so with a new perspective on your relationship with your father. Through the lens of forgiveness and healing, you've gained insight into his struggles, imperfections, and limitations. You've recognized that he, too, is human, navigating life's challenges with his own experiences and burdens. This newfound perspective allows you to release the unrealistic expectations you once held, freeing him and yourself from the cycle of blame.

Closing this journal chapter, you carry a profound transformation—a new perspective on your relationship with your father. Through the lens of forgiveness and healing, you've gained invaluable insight into his struggles, imperfections, and limitations.

Like all of us, you've realized he is fundamentally human, navigating life's challenges with his own experiences and burdens. This newfound perspective extends the compassion and understanding you've cultivated to include him.

This shift in perspective is liberating. It allows you to release the unrealistic expectations that may have previously burdened your relationship. It's an act of grace that sets you and your father free from the cycle of blame and resentment.

As you move forward, remember that this new perspective is a gift—an offering of peace and reconciliation. It doesn't erase the past but transforms how you carry it. It enables you to embrace the complexities of your relationship with a compassionate heart.

With this perspective, you enter a future of emotional liberation and healing. You're no longer bound by the weight of old wounds but empowered by the wisdom and empathy from forgiveness. This is a powerful beginning, a new chapter of your life where you can foster healthier connections and inner peace. Continue to nurture this perspective as you journey toward a future defined by love, growth, and authentic relationships.

A Letter of Forgiveness

Writing a letter of forgiveness to your father is a meaningful step in your healing journey, and I want to honor your courage and resilience. This letter is not just words on paper; it's a powerful symbol of your transformation.

Within the lines of this letter lies the weight of your journey—a journey of self-discovery, self-compassion, and emotional liberation. It reflects the growth you've achieved, the insights you've gained, and the profound healing you've experienced.

By choosing to forgive, you're letting go of the heavy burden of resentment that may have held you captive for so long. It's a declaration of your commitment to living a life untethered by the chains of the past. You're choosing to break free and enter a future where you can thrive without the weight of old wounds.

This letter signifies the closing of one chapter of pain, blame, and hurt. It begins a new narrative defined by self-empowerment, healing, and the freedom to create your desired life. It's a testament to your strength and capacity to rise above adversity.

As you move forward, remember that forgiveness is not a one-time event but an ongoing process. Continue to nurture the seeds of forgiveness within your heart. Embrace the newfound freedom and lightness that forgiveness brings, and let it guide you toward a future filled with love, growth, and authentic connection. Your journey is an inspiration, and I encourage you to keep walking the path of healing with unwavering determination and self-compassion.

In writing this journal, you may have chosen to pen a letter of forgiveness to your father—a letter that carries the weight of your journey, your growth, and your willingness to let go. This letter is a profound gesture, a release of the past, and a declaration of your commitment to living a life untethered by resentment. It signifies the closing of one chapter and the beginning of a new narrative—one defined by self-empowerment, healing, and the freedom to thrive.

A Future of Empowerment

As you embark on the next chapter of your life, know that you carry the invaluable lessons and insights from this transformative journey. The profound changes you've experienced are not an endpoint but the beginning of a lifelong commitment to self, healing, and ongoing growth.

The tools you've cultivated during this journey are like treasures in your arsenal. The power of forgiveness has set you free from the chains of resentment, allowing you to soar unburdened. The resilience of healing has shown you that even in the face of adversity, you possess the strength to overcome and thrive. Embracing accountability has given you the power to shape your narrative and define your future.

With these tools firmly in your grasp, you step into the future with a renewed sense of empowerment. You're not defined by your past wounds but by your capacity to heal and grow. You are the author of your own story, and you have the power to craft a narrative filled with love, authenticity, and boundless possibilities.

Embrace this future with open arms, for it is a future of empowerment. In this journey, you continue to uncover your most authentic self, deepen your connection with others, and thrive in the fullness of your potential. The road ahead may have challenges, but with your newfound strength and wisdom, you are well-prepared to navigate them with grace and resilience. Your healing journey is a testament to your incredible spirit. I encourage you to move forward with unwavering determination, self-compassion, and the belief that your best days are yet to come.

As you enter the next chapter of your life, carry the lessons and insights from this journey. Your transformation is not a finite destination but an ongoing process—a commitment to yourself, healing, and continued growth. With the tools you've cultivated—the power of forgiveness, the resilience of healing, and the strength of accountability—you are equipped to face the future with a renewed sense of empowerment.

A Journey Unveiled

The pages of this journal have served as a canvas upon which you've painted the intricate tapestry of your journey. Each word, each reflection, and each moment of vulnerability has contributed to the masterpiece that is your story. The journey of forgiveness, healing, and self-empowerment is not confined to these pages; it lives within you, shaping your thoughts, actions, and interactions.

As you close this journal, remember that forgiveness is an ongoing practice, healing is a continuous journey, and self-empowerment is a lifelong commitment. The legacy of this journey lives in your choices, relationships, and sense of self-worth. May you carry the lessons of forgiveness and healing with you, allowing them to guide you toward a life of authenticity, compassion, and the unwavering belief that you deserve love, joy, and peace.

The journey you've undertaken is a testament to your strength, your resilience, and your capacity to embrace transformation. It is a journey of profound significance—a journey towards freedom, empowerment, and the discovery of the boundless potential within you.

The journey you've embarked upon is a testament to the remarkable qualities that reside within you. This journey bears witness to your strength, resilience, and unwavering commitment to healing and growth. Through every page of this journal, you've demonstrated the courage to face the shadows of the past and the determination to emerge into the light of self-discovery.

This journey is of profound significance. It's a pilgrimage towards freedom—a liberation from the heavy chains of old wounds and resentments. It's a path to empowerment—realizing your innate strength and capacity to shape your destiny. It's an expedition of self-discovery—an unveiling of the boundless potential that resides within you, waiting to be unleashed.

In the quiet moments of reflection, you've delved deep into your heart and soul, uncovering the hidden gems of self-awareness and self-compassion. You've learned the transformative power of forgiveness, the resilience of healing, and the strength of accountability. These are not just lessons but the keys that unlock the doors to a life defined by authenticity, joy, and fulfillment.

As you stand at this juncture, take a moment to honor yourself for the remarkable journey you've undertaken. Know that your healing and growth are ongoing processes; every step you take is a testament to your unwavering spirit. Embrace the freedom, empowerment, and boundless potential that await you on the horizon. The journey may have had its challenges, but it has also been a source of profound transformation and inner liberation. Continue to walk this path with courage and self-compassion, for the best chapters of your life are yet to be written.

Below Is A List Of All 35 Forgiveness Journals

Written By: Tuniscia Okeke

Available on Amazon and other major bookstores or www.forgivenesslifestyle.com
Instagram: @forgiveness_lifestyle
For bulk orders: info@forgivenesslifestyle.com

Forgiving Yourself

Forgiving Your Body Journal

Accepting the Gift of Forgiveness Journal

Forgiving People Who Reject You Journal

P.S. Forgive Yourself First Journal

Who Do You Struggle To Forgive Journal

Forgiving Your Struggle With Addiction Journal

Forgiving Your Parents

Forgiving Your Mother Journal

Forgiving Your Father Journal

Forgiving Your Parents Journal

Parenthood

Forgiving and Overcoming Mom Guilt Journal

Forgiveness Journal for Fathers

Parents Forgiving Tweens/Teen Journal

Parents Forgiving Adult Children Journal

Family

Forgiving Dead Loved One's Journal

Forgiving Family Secrets Journal

Forgiving The Bullies In Your Family Journal

Forgiving Your Siblings Journal

Marriage

Forgiving Your Wife Journal

Forgiving Your Husband Journal

Forgiving Your Mother-
In-Law Journal

Romantic Relationships

Forgiving Your Ex Journal

Forgiving The "New"
Woman Journal

Teens & Millennials

Forgiveness Journals for Teens

Forgiveness Journal
for Millennials

Religion

Forgiving God Journal

Forgiving Church People Journal

Blended Family

Forgiving A Co-Parent Journal

Forgiveness Journal
for Stepmothers

Forgiving Your
Stepmother Journal

Forgiving Your Stepkids
Mom Journal

Relationships

Forgiving Your Abuser Journal

Forgiving Friends Journal

Business/Finances

Forgiveness In Business Journal

Forgiving People At
Work Journal

Forgiving Past Money
Mistakes Journal

Sending you loving energy as you
forgive, heal, and grow.
www.forgivenesslifestyle.com

Thank You

Gratitude is the thread that weaves connections, and at this moment, I extend my most profound appreciation to those whose unwavering support and love have been the foundation of this 35-journal writing journey and beyond.

To my beloved husband, your unwavering confidence and support during our marriage and this writing project have been my anchor. Thank you for your belief in me. It has been a constant source of inspiration. Your love and presence in my life make my soul smile.

Your honesty and vulnerability to my mother led to this beautiful healing journey. Your transparency has supported my healing and given me the strength to support others on their transformational journey. I will forever be grateful for your courage to tell the truth.

My dear daughter, Shantia Dajah, your reminder to give myself grace has been a guiding light. Your wisdom transcends your years. You make my heart smile.

To my incredible son, Damien, your encouragement and motivation have fueled my determination to embark on this transformative journey. Your presence in my life is a source of boundless joy.

To Ike, my dynamic youngest son, your cheering from the sidelines has been a source of motivation and warmth. Your enthusiasm lights up my days.

My sister, Tanniedra, your unwavering belief in me and our brainstorming sessions have been invaluable. You are truly a gift.

Little sister, Jazmin, your willingness to share your experiences and vulnerability has touched my heart deeply. Your courage is inspiring.

To my "business bestie," Martha Banks Hall, the Creator of Vision Words, your prayers, encouraging texts, and our deep explorations of thoughts have been a source of clarity and growth to help me birth this project.

Denise, my beautiful friend, "The Fertility Godmother," your enthusiastic voice memos have made me feel like a rock star. Your presence has been a pillar of my strength.

To Thuy, I'm deeply grateful for your accountability and sisterhood, and I hold you as the beautiful gift you are close to my heart.

To Georgette and Cristal, your cheers have lifted my spirits. Your presence in my life is a blessing.

You all hold a special place in my heart, and I thank you from the depths of my soul for being a part of my journey.

Made in the USA
Middletown, DE
15 October 2023

40779062R00133